Ernest Renan, Charles Beard

Lectures on the Influence of the Institutions

thought and culture of Rome, on Christianity and the development of the Catholic

church. Fourth Edition

Ernest Renan, Charles Beard

Lectures on the Influence of the Institutions
thought and culture of Rome, on Christianity and the development of the Catholic church.
Fourth Edition

ISBN/EAN: 9783337262952

Printed in Europe, USA, Canada, Australia, Japan

Cover: Foto ©Lupo / pixelio.de

More available books at **www.hansebooks.com**

THE HIBBERT LECTURES,
1880.

ON THE INFLUENCE OF

THE INSTITUTIONS, THOUGHT AND CULTURE

OF

ROME,

ON

CHRISTIANITY AND THE DEVELOPMENT OF THE CATHOLIC CHURCH.

BY

ERNEST RENAN,
OF THE FRENCH ACADEMY.

TRANSLATED BY CHARLES BEARD, B.A.

FOURTH EDITION.

WILLIAMS AND NORGATE,
14, HENRIETTA STREET, COVENT GARDEN, LONDON;
20, SOUTH FREDERICK STREET, EDINBURGH;
AND 7, BROAD STREET, OXFORD.

1898.

LONDON:
PRINTED BY C. GREEN AND SON,
178, STRAND.

PREFACE.

THE "Hibbert Lectures" have been instituted for the purpose of providing a series of Lessons on the most important chapters of the History of Religion. It is in this connection that M. Max Müller has treated of the general development of religion in India, that M. Le Page Renouf has spoken of the religious function of Egypt. They form in some sort a Chair of the Comparative History of Religion, but a Chair which is occupied every year by a new Professor, who speaks only of that which he has made the subject of special study. I therefore felt myself deeply honoured when the Trustees of this useful Institution invited me to continue a teaching so worthily begun. I had long desired to see England, and to clasp the hand of my many English friends. I accepted the invitation; and certainly the kind welcome which I met with from a nation which has always inspired me with the greatest esteem and the highest sympathy, has been one of the rewards of my life. The spectacle of a proud and strong people, in the enjoyment of the largest liberty which humanity has hitherto been able to make its own, has filled me with a lively joy, and has confirmed me in the conviction that the future of Europe, despite many a passing storm, belongs to an ideal of light and peace.

Our society is sceptical only in appearance: it has its own dogma, and that an excellent one, Liberty, respect for the mind. This dogma will conquer every other; only we must beware of believing that laws and decrees can assist its triumphs. Let Liberty alone: fanatics fear her more than they fear persecution: in her own unaided strength she knows how to overcome her enemies.

E. R.

Paris, *June,* 1880.

TABLE OF CONTENTS.

LECTURE I.
	PAGE
IN WHAT SENSE IS CHRISTIANITY THE WORK OF ROME?	1

LECTURE II.
THE LEGEND OF THE ROMAN CHURCH: PETER AND PAUL   39

LECTURE III.
ROME, THE CENTRE OF GROWING ECCLESIASTICAL AUTHORITY   101

LECTURE IV.
ROME, THE CAPITAL OF CATHOLICISM   .   .   .   145

DR. MARTINEAU'S ADDRESS   207

LECTURE I.

IN WHAT SENSE IS CHRISTIANITY THE WORK OF ROME?

LECTURE I.

IN WHAT SENSE IS CHRISTIANITY THE WORK OF ROME?

It gave me both pride and pleasure to receive from the Trustees of this noble Institution an invitation to continue in this place a course of instruction begun by my illustrious brother and friend, Max Müller, a course the usefulness of which will become more manifest from day to day. A broad and honest idea always bears fruit. It is now more than thirty years since the venerable Robert Hibbert left behind him a legacy, intended to promote the progress of enlightened Christianity, which in his view was inseparable from the progress of science and reason. Wisely interpreted, this foundation has become, in the hands of intelligent administrators, the occasion of Lectures upon all the chief epochs of the religious history of humanity. Why—the promoters of this reform have rightly said—why should not the method which has approved itself in all other departments of intellectual culture, be applicable in the domain of religion also? Why should the pursuit of truth, without care of consequences, be dangerous in theology, when it is accepted by all in the domain of the social and natural sciences? You have believed in truth, and you are right. There is but one truth; and it is to show ourselves something less than respectful to revelation, to confess that, in regard to it, criticism is compelled to modify the severity of its methods. No; truth can dispense with politeness. I have been happy to respond to your invitation, for I understand duty to the truth exactly as you do. Like you, I should think that I was insulting truth if I allowed that it was necessary to treat it with a certain indulgence. I believe, as you do, that the worship which man owes to the ideal is research,—scientific, independent, indifferent to results; and that the true method of rendering homage to truth is to pursue it unremittingly, and with the firm resolve to sacrifice everything to it.

Your desire is, that these Lectures should combine to form one great historical presentation of the efforts which the human race has made to resolve the problems which surround it, and which determine its destiny. In the present condition of the human mind, no one can hope to resolve these problems; and we justly suspect all dogmatism, simply because it is dogmatic. We are willing to admit that a religious or philosophical system may and even must contain a certain element of absolute truth; but we deny, even before we have examined its claims, that it can possibly contain absolute truth itself. What we love is history. History, well written, is always good. For even if it could be proved that man, in his efforts to lay hold of the infinite, had been pursuing a chimera, the story of his attempts, always more noble than successful, could not fail to be useful. It proves that, in very truth, man, in virtue of his aspirations, emerges from the circle of his bounded life; it shows what energy he has put forth for the pure love of the good and the true; it teaches us to esteem him—this poor disinherited creature—who, in addition to the sufferings which nature lays upon him, lays upon himself the torment of the unknown, the torment of doubt, the hard resistances of virtue, the abstinences of a scrupulous conscience, the voluntary punishments of the ascetic. And is all this simple loss? This effort, unceasingly renewed, to attain the unattainable, is it as vain as the infant's pursuit of the always retreating object of its desire? I can hardly believe it; and the faith which escapes me when I examine in detail each of the religious systems which divide the world among them, in part returns to me when I reflect upon them as a whole. All religions may be defective and partial; but religion is none the less a divine element in humanity, and the mark of a superior fate. No; they have not laboured in vain, those great founders, those reformers, those prophets of every age, who have protested against the delusive evidence of a fatality which closes us round, who have dashed themselves against the wall of a gross materialism, who have consumed their thought, who have given their life for the accomplishment of a mission which the spirit of their age laid upon them. If the fact of the existence of martyrs does not prove that truth is the exclusive possession of this or that sect (and every sect can adduce a rich martyrology), yet, taken in the general, it shows that religious zeal corresponds to some mysterious reality. Such as we are, we are all sons of the martyrs. Those who speak most freely of scepticism are often the men of the deepest and the sincerest convictions. Those who in your own country have founded religious and political liberty; those who have established throughout the whole of Europe freedom of thought and of research; those who have laboured to improve the lot of mankind; those who doubtless will yet find the means of improving it still more,—all have expiated or will expiate their good deeds; for labour for the happiness of humanity is never recompensed. And still they will never lack imitators. There will never be wanting to take up their work men who cannot be stayed or turned aside, men possessed by the Divine Spirit, who will sacrifice their personal interests to truth and justice. Let them alone; they have chosen the better part. Something assures me that he who, hardly knowing why, has, out of simple nobleness of nature, chosen for himself in this world the essentially unproductive function of doing good, is the truly wise man, and has discerned, with more sagacity than the egotist, the legitimate employment of life.

I.

You have asked of me that, in your presence, I should retrace one of those pages of history which put the thoughts that I have just uttered in the clearest light. The origins of Christianity form the most heroic episode of the history of humanity. Never will man display more self-devotion or a larger love of the ideal, than in the hundred and fifty years which rolled away between the sweet Galilean vision under Tiberius and the death of Marcus Aurelius. Never was the religious consciousness more eminently creative; never did it lay down with more absolute authority the law of the future. This extraordinary movement, with which no other can be compared, came out of the heart of Judaism. But it is doubtful whether Judaism alone would have conquered the world. For this, it was needful that the young and hardy school which sprang from it, should be bold enough to repudiate the greater part of the Mosaic ritual. It was, above all, needful that the new movement should transfer itself to the Greek and Latin world, and there, awaiting the barbarians, should become, as it were, a leaven in the midst of those European races, by means of which humanity accomplishes its destiny. What a noble subject will *he* have, who some day will undertake the task of expounding to you the share of Greece in this great common work! You have asked me to explain to you the part of Rome. There is a sense in which, in point of time, the action of Rome comes first. It is only in the earlier part of the third century that the Greek mind, in the persons of Clement of Alexandria and of Origen, really laid hold of Christianity. I hope to prove to you that in the second century Rome exercised a decisive influence on the Church of Jesus.

In one sense, Rome has propagated religion in the

world, as it has propagated civilization, as it has spread the idea of a central government, extending over a large part of the earth. But, in the same way as the civilization which Rome propagated was not the petty, narrow, austere culture of ancient Latium, but the grand and large civilization which Greece had created, so the religion to which it finally lent its support was not the mean superstition which satisfied the rude and primitive settlers on the Palatine; it was Judaism—that is to say, precisely the religion which Rome most hated and despised, the religion which, two or three times over, she believed that she had finally vanquished, and supplanted by her own national worship.

This old faith of Latium, which for ages satisfied a race whose intellectual and moral wants were limited, and with whom manners and social bearing almost held the place of religion, was a somewhat pitiful thing.[1] A more false conception of Deity is nowhere to be found: in the Roman, as in the majority of the old Italian cults, prayer is a magic

---

[1] See the excellent exposition of M. Gaston Boissier, *La Religion Romaine*, Vol. i. p. 1 et seq. : Paris, 1874.

formula, producing its effect by its own inherent quality, and without reference to the moral disposition of the worshipper: no one prays except for his own private advantage: there are registers called *indigitamenta*, containing the list of gods who provide for all the wants of men. Worshippers must beware of mistakes: if the god is not addressed by his true name, that by which he is pleased to be invoked, he is capable of misunderstanding or of thwarting the petition. Now these gods, who are in some sort the forces of the world, are innumerable. There is a little god who causes the infant to utter its first cry (*vaticanus*); there is another who presides over its first word (*fabulinus*); one who teaches the baby to eat (*educa*), another to drink (*potina*); finally, one who keeps it quiet in its cradle (*cuba*). In short, the good woman in Petronius was right when, speaking of Campania, she said: "This country is so peopled with divinities, that a god is easier to find in it than a man." In addition to all this, there is an endless series of allegories or deified abstractions: Fear, Cough, Fever, Male Fortune, Patrician Modesty, Plebeian Modesty, the Safety of the Age, the

Genius of the Custom-house,[1] and above all (mark—this is in truth the great God of Rome), the Safety of the Roman People. It was, in the full force of the word, a civil religion. It was essentially the religion of the State: there was no priesthood distinct from State functions: the State was the true God of Rome. The father had over the son the right of life and death; but if the son held the least important office, and the father met him in the road, he dismounted from his horse and bowed down before him.

The consequence of this essentially political character of Roman religion was, that it always remained aristocratic. A man became pontiff as he became prætor or consul: when he was a candidate for religious office, he underwent no examination, he passed no period of probation in a seminary, he was not asked if he had an ecclesiastical vocation. He proved that he had served his country well, and had fought bravely in this or that battle. There was no sacerdotal spirit: these civil pontiffs con-

---

[1] Or rather, of Indirect Taxes, GENIO PORTORII PUBLICI. *Ann. de l'Inst. Arch. de Rome*, 1868, pp. 8, 9.

tinued to be what they had been, cold, practical men, without the slightest idea that their functions at all cut them off from the rest of the world. In every respect the religion of Rome was the reverse of a theocracy. The Civil Law regulates actions; it does not occupy itself with ideas; and so one result of Roman religion was, that Rome never had the faintest conception of dogma. The exact observance of rites compels the Deity, who, if the petition be presented in proper form, has no inquiry to make into piety or the feelings of the heart. More than this: devoutness is a defect; it implies a dangerous exaltation in the popular mind. Calm, order, regularity—this is what is wanted. Anything beyond this is excess (*superstitio*). Cato absolutely forbids that slaves should be allowed to entertain any sentiment of piety. "Know," he says, "that the master sacrifices for the whole household." Can anything be more civil, lay, peremptory, than this? Men must not fail in what is due to the gods; but they must not give them more than their due: that is the *superstitio* which the true Roman abhorred as much as he abhorred impiety.

Could there be, I ask you, a religion less capable than this of becoming the religion of the human race? Not only was entrance to the priesthood forbidden to plebeians; they were shut out from public worship. In that long struggle for civil equality which fills Roman history, religion is the great argument alleged against the friends of revolution. "How could you possibly become prætor or consul?" it was said. "You do not possess the right of taking the auspices." And thus the people had very little attachment to religion. Every popular victory is, as we should say, followed by an anti-clerical reaction. On the other hand, the aristocracy always remained faithful to a worship which gave a divine sanction to its privileges.

The question arose in a much more decisive shape when the Roman people, in the exercise of their masculine and patriotic virtues, had conquered all the nations on the shores of the Mediterranean. What interest could an African, a Gaul, a Syrian take in a worship which concerned only a very small number of haughty and often tyrannical families? Everywhere the local cults continued to exist; but Augustus, who was even more a religious organizer than a great politician, gave universal currency to the Roman idea by instituting the worship of Rome. The altars of Rome and of Augustus became the centre of an hierarchical organization of flamens and Augustal sevirs,[1] which, to a much greater extent than is commonly supposed, furnished the basis for the division of dioceses and ecclesiastical provinces. Augustus admits all local gods as Lares: more than this, he permits that to the number of Lares in each house, at each crossway, should be added another Lar, the Genius of the Emperor. Thanks to this confraternity, all local gods, all private divinities, became Augustal gods. It was an admirable promotion for them. But this great attempt to produce a religion of the Roman State, was evidently incapable of satisfying the religious wants of the heart. And, besides, there was one God, who could in no wise accommodate himself to this fraternal equality—the God of the Jews. It was impossible to pass off Jehovah as a Lar, and to associate with Him the Genius of the Emperor.

---

[1] That is, colleges of priests, consisting of six members.

The moment this was perceived, it was plain that a battle would have to be fought between the Roman State and this uncompromising and refractory God, who did not lend himself to the accommodating transformations exacted by the policy of the age.

Here, then, is the most extraordinary of historical phenomena, the highest expression of the irony of history—that the worship which Rome has spread abroad in the world is by no means that of the old Jupiter Capitolinus or Latiaris; still less the worship of Augustus or of the Genius of the Empire; it is the worship of Jehovah. It is Judaism in its Christian form that Rome has unconsciously propagated, and that with such vigour, as, after a certain time has elapsed, to make Romanism and Christianity almost synonymous terms.

Certainly, I must repeat, it is more than doubtful whether pure Judaism, the Judaism which was developed in a Talmudic form and which still preserves so much of its power, would ever have had so extraordinary a fortune. The Jewish propaganda was made by means of Christianity. But we are altogether ignorant of religious history—a fact which I hope some other lecturer will prove to you at a future time—if we do not lay it down as a fundamental principle, that Christianity at its origin is no other than Judaism, with its fertile principles of almsgiving and charity, with its absolute faith in the future of humanity, with that joy of heart of which Judaism has always held the secret—and denuded only of the distinctive observances and features which had been invented to give a character of its own to the peculiar religion of the children of Israel.

II.

If we study the progress of primitive Christian missions, we shall find that they all take a Western direction, or, to put it in another way, that they find both theatre and limit in the Roman Empire. With exception of some small portions of the territory, subject to the Arsacidæ, between the Euphrates and the Tigris, the Parthian Empire received no Christian missions in the first century. The Tigris was, on the side of the East, a boundary which Christianity did not pass till the age of the Sassanidæ. This fact, of capital importance, was determined by two great causes, the Mediterranean Sea and the Roman Empire.

For a thousand years the Mediterranean had been the great highway where all civilizations and all ideas had met and mingled. The Romans, in clearing it of pirates, had made it an unequalled means of communication. It was, in some sort, the railway of those times. A numerous coasting marine facilitated intercourse along the shores of this great lake. The comparative security offered by the roads of the Empire, the protection afforded by public functionaries, the diffusion of the Jews throughout all the shores of the Mediterranean, the use of the Greek language in the Eastern half of that sea, the unity of civilization which first the Greeks and afterwards the Romans had there created, made the map of the Empire the map also of the countries reserved for Christian missions and destined to become Christian. The Roman world became the Christian world; and there is a sense in which we may say that the founders of the Empire were the founders of the Christian monarchy, or at least that they determined its outline and area. Every province conquered by the Roman Empire was a province conquered for Christianity. Think of the Apostles in face of an

Asia Minor, a Greece, an Italy, divided into a hundred little republics; of a Gaul, a Spain, an Africa, in possession of old national institutions—and it is no longer possible to conceive of their success, or even to understand how their project could have had its birth. The unity of the Empire was the condition precedent of any great religious proselytism which should set itself above nationalities. In the fourth century the Empire felt this fully: it became Christian: it saw that Christianity was the religion which it had made without knowing it, the religion bounded by its frontiers, identified with itself, capable of infusing into it a second life. The Church, on its side, became completely Roman, and has remained up to our own day, as it were, a remnant of the Empire. Throughout all the Middle Ages, the Church is no other than the old Rome, regaining its authority over the barbarians who have conquered it,—imposing upon them its decretals, as it formerly imposed its laws,—governing them by its cardinals, as it once governed them by its imperial legates and its proconsuls.

In creating, then, its vast empire, Rome laid down

the material condition of the propagation of Christianity. Above all, it created the moral state which supplied to the new doctrine both atmosphere and medium. In killing politics all over the world, it created what we may call socialism and religion. After the frightful wars which for ages had torn the earth in pieces, the Empire was an era of prosperity and welfare such as had never before been known; we may even add, without paradox, that it was an era of liberty. On the one hand, liberty of trade and of industry—a liberty of which the Greek republics had no conception—became possible. On the other, liberty of thought gained greatly by the new government. This is a kind of liberty which often finds it more advantageous to treat with kings or princes than with jealous and narrow-minded citizens. The ancient republics did not possess it. Without it, the Greeks—thanks to the incomparable power of their genius—accomplished great things; but we must not forget that Athens undoubtedly had an Inquisition of her own.[1] The King Archon

---

[1] Study the character of Euthyphron in Plato.

was the Inquisitor: the Royal Porch, the Holy Office whence issued the accusations of "impiety." Arraignments of this nature were very numerous: it is the kind of case which we meet with oftenest in the Attic orators. Not only philosophical crimes, such as the denial of God or of Providence, but the slightest offences against municipal cults, the preaching of foreign religions, the most puerile infractions of the scrupulous legislation of the Mysteries, were punished with death. The gods whom Aristophanes scoffed at on the stage, sometimes slew the scoffers. They killed Socrates, they all but killed Alcibiades. Anaxagoras, Protagoras, Diagoras of Melos, Prodicus of Ceos, Stilpo, Aristotle, Theophrastus, Aspasia, Euripides, were more or less seriously disquieted. Liberty of thought was, in fact, the child of the dynasties which were founded upon the Macedonian conquests. It was the Attali, the Ptolemies, who first gave thinkers the freedom which none of the old republics had accorded to them. The Roman Empire continued the same tradition. It is true that under the Empire more than one arbitrary decree was directed against the philosophers, but it was in every case the result of their meddling with politics. We search in vain, in the collection of Roman laws before Constantine, for any enactment aimed at free thought, or in the history of the Emperors for a prosecution of abstract doctrine. Not a single *savant* was disturbed. Men whom the Middle Ages would have burned—such as Galen, Lucian, Plotinus—lived in peace, protected by the law. The Empire inaugurated a period of liberty, in so far as it abolished the absolute sovereignty of the family, the city, the tribe, and replaced or modified these sovereignties by that of the State. Now, absolute power is vexatious in precise proportion to the narrowness of the area over which it is exercised. The old republics, the feudal system, tyrannized over the individual much more than the State has ever done. It is true that the Roman Empire, at various epochs, sternly persecuted Christianity, but nevertheless it did not arrest its progress. But the republics would have made it impossible: even Judaism, but for the pressure of Roman authority, would have been strong enough to stifle it. It was the Roman magistrates who prevented the Pharisees from killing Christianity.

Large conceptions of universal fraternity, for the most part the issue of Stoicism, as well as a kind of general sentiment of humanity, were the product of the less strict government and the less exclusive education to which the individual was subjected. Men dreamed of a new era and of new worlds.[1] The wealth of the community was great, and, in spite of the imperfectness of current economical doctrines, ease and comfort were wide-spread. Public morals were not what they are often supposed to have been. In Rome, it is true, every vice flaunted itself with revolting cynicism: the public games, especially, had introduced a frightful corruption. Certain countries—for example, Egypt—had descended to the lowest moral depth. But in most of the provinces existed a middle class, among whom kindness, conjugal fidelity, domestic virtue, probity, were general.[2] Is there anywhere an ideal of family life,

---

[1] Virgil, *Ecl.* iv. Seneca, *Medea*, 375 et seq.

[2] The epitaphs of women contain the most touching expressions. "Mater omnium hominum, parens omnibus subveniens," in Renier, *Inscr. de l'Algérie*, No. 1987. Comp. *ibid.* No. 2756. Mommsen, *Inscr. R.N.* No. 1431. "Duobus virtutis et

among the honest inhabitants of small towns, more charming than that of which Plutarch has left us the picture? What goodnatured kindness! what gentleness of manners! what chaste and amiable simplicity! Chæronea was evidently not the only spot where life was so pure and so innocent.

The habits of the people, even elsewhere than at Rome, had still some taint of cruelty—either a remnant of ancient manners, which were everywhere sanguinary, or a special result of Roman hardness. But there was progress in this respect too. What sweet and pure sentiment, what mood of melancholy tenderness, has not found its finest expression in the verses of Virgil or of Tibullus? The world was becoming more supple, losing its old stiffness, acquiring softness and sensibility. Maxims of humanity were gaining currency: equality, the abstract idea of the rights of man, was boldly preached by Stoic-

---

castitatis exemplis:" *Not. et Mém. de la Soc. de Constantine*, 1865, p. 158. " Affectionis plena erga omnes homines:" Le Blant, *Inscr. Chr. de la Gaule*, pp. 172, 173. "Ob egregiam ad omnes homines mansuetudinem." See the inscr. of Urbanilla, in Guérin, *Voy. Archéol. dans la rég. de Tunis*, i. 289; and the delicious inscription, Orelli, No. 4618.

ism. Woman was becoming more and more mistress of herself: humaner methods of treating slaves came into vogue:[1] Seneca took his meals with his.[2] The slave is no longer that necessarily grotesque and mischievous being whom the Latin Comedy brought upon the stage to excite the laughter of the audience, and whom Cato recommended should be treated as a beast of burthen. Now, times are completely changed. The slave is morally equal to his master: he is allowed to be capable of virtue, of faithfulness, of devotion; and he gives proofs that he is so. Prejudices as to noble birth were passing away. Even under the worst Emperors, many just and humane laws were enacted. Tiberius was an able financier: he founded a *Credit Foncier*[3] upon excellent principles. Nero introduced into the system of taxation, which up to that time had been barbarous and unjust,

---

[1] Tacit. *Ann.* xiv. 42 et seq. Sueton. *Claudius*, 25. *Dio Cassius*, lx. 29. Plin. *Epist.* viii. 16. Inscript. of Lanuvium, col. 2, lines 1—4 (in Mommsen, *De Coll. et Sodal. Rom.*). Seneca Rhet. *Controv.* iii. 21, viii. 6. Seneca Phil. Epist. xlvii. *De Benef.* iii. 18 et seq. Columella, *De re rusticâ*, i. 8. Plutarch, *Cato the Elder*, 5; *De Irâ*, 11.

[2] Epist. xlvii. 13.   [3] Tacit. *Ann.* vi. 17; conf. iv. 6.

improvements which shame even our own age.¹ The progress of legislation was not inconsiderable, although capital punishment was still stupidly frequent. Almsgiving, the love of the poor, universal sympathy, came to be looked upon as virtues.²

III.

At the same time, I understand and share the indignation of sincere liberals against a system of government which subjected the world to a frightful despotism. But is it our fault that the wants of humanity are diverse, its aspirations many, its aims contradictory? Politics are not everything here

---

¹ Tacit. *Ann.* xiii. 50, 51. Sueton. *Nero*, 10.

² Epitaph of the Jeweller Evhodus (hominis boni, misericordis, amantis pauperes): *Corpus Inscr. Lat.* No. 1027. Inscription of the age of Augustus. (Conf. Egger, *Mém. d'Hist. anc. et de phil.* 351 et seq.). Perrot, *Expl. de la Galatie,* &c. 118, 119 (πτωχοὺς φιλέοντα). Funeral oration of Matidia by Hadrian: *Mem. of the Acad. of Berlin,* 1863, p. 489. Mommsen, *Inscr. Regni Neap.* Nos. 1431, 2868, 4880. Seneca Rhet. *Controv.* i. 1, iii. 19, iv. 27, viii. 6. Seneca Phil. *De Clem.* ii. 5, 6; *De Benef.* i. 1, ii. 11, iv. 14, vii. 31. Conf. Le Blant, *Inscr. Chr. de la Gaule,* ii. 23 et seq. Orelli, No. 4657. Fea, *Framm. de' Fasti Consul.* p. 90. R. Garrucci, *Cimitero degli ant. Ebrei,* p. 44.

below. What the world wanted, after the frightful butcheries of antiquity, was gentleness, humanity. Of heroism, it had had enough: those masculine goddesses, for ever brandishing a spear from the height of an Acropolis, no longer awoke any sentiment. The earth, as in the days of Cadmus, had devoured its noblest sons: the finest races of Greece had perished by mutual slaughter: Peloponnesus was a desert. The gentle voice of Virgil well expressed the general cry of humanity—Peace! Pity!

The establishment of Christianity answered to this cry of all tender and weary spirits. But Christianity could be born and spread abroad only at an epoch when men had no longer a native country. If there is anything which the founders of the Church entirely lacked, it was patriotism. They are not cosmopolitan, for the whole planet is to them a place of exile: they are idealists in the most absolute sense of the word. A country is a composite whole, made up of soul and body. Remembrances, usages, legends, misfortunes, hopes, common regrets —these are the soul; the soil, the race, the language, the mountains, the rivers, the characteristic produc-

tions, are the body. But from all this no men were
ever more completely detached than the first Christians. They had no affection for Judea: at the end
of a few years they have forgotten Galilee: the glory
of Greece and of Rome is to them matter of indifference. The countries in which Christianity first
established itself—Syria, Cyprus, Asia Minor—no
longer recollected a time at which they had been
free. Greece and Rome still cherished a strong
feeling of nationality. But in Rome, patriotism
lived only in the bosom of a few families; in Greece,
except at Corinth, a city which, after its destruction
by Mummius and its rebuilding by Cæsar, was a
collection of people of every race and kind, Christianity did not prosper. The really Greek countries,
then as now very jealous, very much absorbed in
the recollection of their past, lent themselves but
little to the new preaching, and were never enthusiastically Christian. On the contrary, those soft,
gay, voluptuous lands of Asia, of Syria, lands of
pleasure, of carelessness, of easy morals, accustomed
to receive life and regulation from without, had
neither pride to give up nor traditions to forget.

The oldest capitals of Christianity—Antioch, Ephesus, Thessalonica, Corinth, Rome—were, if I may use the phrase, common cities, cities after the fashion of modern Alexandria, where all races flowed together, and where the marriage between man and the soil, which makes the nation, was entirely dissolved.

The importance given to social questions is always in an inverse ratio to the strength of political preoccupations. Socialism gets the upper hand when patriotism grows weak. Christianity was that breaking forth of social and religious ideas which became inevitable as soon as Augustus had put an end to political struggles. Like Islam, a universal religion, Christianity must be, in its essence, the enemy of nationalities. How many ages, how many schisms have been necessary, before National Churches could be founded in connection with a religion which was from the first the denial of any earthly country, which was born at a time when cities and citizens had alike ceased to exist, and which the old, strong, rigid republics of Greece and of Rome would most certainly have cast out as a poison that would slay the State!

And this was one of the causes of the greatness of the new religion. Humanity is a many-sided, changeful thing, urged this way and that by opposing desires. Country is great, and holy are the heroes of Marathon and Thermopylæ. But, nevertheless, country is not everything here below. We are men and sons of God, before we are Frenchmen or Germans. The kingdom of God—that eternal dream which will never be torn from the heart of man—is the protest against all that in patriotism is too exclusive. The organization of humanity, with a view to its moral improvement and its highest happiness, is a legitimate idea. But the State understands, and can understand, only the organization of egotism. Nor is this a matter of indifference, for egotism is the most powerful of human motives and the easiest to set in motion. But it is not enough. The governments who have started with the hypothesis that man is wholly made up of sordid instincts, have been self-deceived. To him who belongs to a great race, self-devotion is as natural as egotism. And religion is the organization of self-devotion. Let no one, therefore, hope to dispense with religion and religious associations. Each step in advance made by modern society renders this want more imperious. A great increase and deepening of religious sentiment was thus a consequence of the Roman peace established by Augustus: Augustus felt it: but what satisfaction, I ask, of the religious wants which had been called forth, was afforded by the institutions which Rome believed to be eternal? Surely, hardly any. All these ancient worships, while very different in their origin, had one feature in common—an equal inability to develop a theological instruction, a practical morality, an edifying preaching, a pastoral ministry which should be really advantageous to the people. The pagan temple was in no degree what the synagogue and the church were at their best period: I mean the common home, the school, the hostelry, the almshouse, the shelter where the poor sought refuge. It was a cold *cella* into which men went but seldom, and where they learned nothing. The affectation which induced the Roman patricians to distinguish "religion"—that is to say, their own worship—from "superstition," which was the worship of strangers, appears to us puerile. All pagan cults were essentially superstitious. The peasant of our own day, who drops a coin into the box of a miraculous chapel, who asks the aid of a particular saint for his oxen or his horses, who drinks a certain water to cure a special disease, is, in so far, pagan. Almost all our superstitions are the remains of a religion anterior to Christianity, and which Christianity has not been able entirely to root out. If at the present day we wished to recover a living image of paganism, we should have to look for it in some village lying forgotten in the depths of a country district altogether behind the times.

As the only guardians of the pagan cults were interested sacristans and a variable popular tradition, they could not fail to degenerate into adulation. Augustus, though with some reserve, permitted himself to be worshipped in the provinces. Tiberius allowed the ignoble rivalry of the Asian towns, as to which should have the honour of building him a temple, to be decided in his own presence.[1] The

---

[1] Tacit. *Ann.* iv. 55, 56. Conf. Valer. Max. prol.

extravagant impieties of Caligula called forth no reaction: beyond the limits of Judaism, not a single priest was found who cared to resist such follies. Sprung for the most part from a primitive worship of natural forces, repeatedly transformed by popular imagination and admixture of every kind, pagan religions were limited by their own past. It was impossible to get out of them, what was never in them,— Theism, edification. The Fathers of the Church make us smile when they hold up to reprobation the misdeeds of Saturn as the father of a family, of Jupiter as a husband. But certainly it was more ridiculous still to make Jupiter (that is to say, the atmosphere) into a moral God who enjoins, forbids, recompenses, punishes. In a world which aspired to possess a catechism, what could be made of a worship like that of Venus, which, having its origin in an ancient social necessity of the first Phœnician navigations of the Mediterranean, became, as time went on, an outrage upon what was continually more and more regarded as the essence of religion?

This is the explanation of the singular attraction which, about the beginning of the Christian era, drew the populations of the ancient world to the religions of the East. These religions had something deeper in them than those of Greece and Rome: they addressed themselves more fully to the religious sentiment. Almost all of them stood in some relation to the condition of the soul in another life, and it was believed that they held the warrant of immortality. Hence the favour in which the Thracian and Sabazian mysteries, the *thiasi* and the confraternities of all kinds, were held. It was not so chilly in these little circles, where men pressed closely together, as in the great icy world of that day. Little religions, like the worship of Psyche, whose sole object was consolation for human mortality, had a momentary prevalence. The beautiful Egyptian worships, which hid a real emptiness beneath a great splendour of ritual, counted devotees in every part of the Empire. Isis and Serapis had altars even in the ends of the world. A visitor to the ruins of Pompeii might be tempted to believe that the principal worship which obtained there was that of Isis. These little Egyptian temples had their assiduous worshippers, among whom were many of the same class as the friends of Catullus and Tibullus.[1] There was a morning service: a kind of mass, celebrated by a priest, shorn and beardless: there were sprinklings of holy water: possibly benediction in the evening. All this occupied, amused, soothed. What could any one want more?

But it was, above all, the Mithraic worship which in the second and third centuries attained an extraordinary prevalence. I sometimes permit myself to say that, if Christianity had not carried the day, Mithraicism would have become the religion of the world. It had its mysterious meetings: its chapels, which bore a strong resemblance to little churches. It forged a very lasting bond of brotherhood between its initiates: it had a Eucharist, a Supper so like the Christian mysteries, that good Justin Martyr, the Apologist, can find only one explanation of the apparent identity, namely, that Satan, in order to deceive the human race, determined to imitate the Christian ceremonies, and so stole them.[2] A Mithraic

---

[1] See Boissier, *Relig. Rom.* pp. 374 et seq.

[2] Justin, *Apol.* i. 66; *Dial.* 70, 78. Celsus, in Origen, *Contra Celsum,* vi. 22.

LECTURE II.

THE LEGEND OF THE ROMAN CHURCH:
PETER AND PAUL.

LECTURE II.

THE LEGEND OF THE ROMAN CHURCH: PETER AND PAUL.

IN our last Lecture we attempted to describe the difficult situation in regard to all religious questions in which the Roman Empire found itself in the first century. In the vast collection of peoples of which the Empire was made up, existed highly developed religious wants, a genuine moral progress, which gave birth to the desire of a pure worship, without superstitious practices or bloody sacrifices; a tendency to Monotheism, the effect of which was to make the old mythological tales ridiculous; a general sentiment of sympathy and charity, which inspired the wish for association, the need of meeting for mutual prayer and consolation and help, and to assure oneself that after death brethren would lay one in the grave and celebrate a friendly meal in one's remembrance. Asia Minor, Greece, Syria, Egypt, contained masses of poor people, very respectable in their way, humble and without distinction, but disgusted with the spectacle offered to the world by the Roman aristocracy, and full of horror at those hideous performances of the amphitheatre in which Rome had made her executions a public amusement. There arose an immense protest of the moral consciousness of the human race, and there was no priest to become its interpreter, no God with pity in his heart to answer the sighs of poor, suffering humanity. Slavery, in spite of the remonstrances of the wise, was still very hard. Claudius thought that he had done a very humane thing in enacting that the master who had turned out of his house an old and sick slave, should lose all right of property in him if the poor wretch should chance to recover. Who could think that these gods without bowels, the offspring of primeval joy and imagination, had any remedies for such evils? Men wanted a Father in heaven, who should take count of their efforts and assure them a recompence. Men wanted a future of righteousness, in which the earth should belong to the feeble and the poor; they wanted the assurance that human suffering is not all loss, but that beyond this sad horizon, dimmed by tears, are happy plains where sorrow shall one day find its consolation.

This was exactly what Judaism had. In its institution of the synagogue—and do not forget that out of the synagogue arose the church—it reduced association to practice in a more powerful form than had ever before been the case. Its worship was, at least in appearance, pure Deism. It had no images. For idols it had nothing but contempt and sarcasm. But what more than all else characterized the Jew, was his confident belief in a brilliant and happy future for humanity. Having no definite idea of the immortality of the soul, or of recompence and retribution in another life, the Jew, taught by the old prophets, was, as it were, intoxicated with the sentiment of justice. And he desired justice here below, upon this earth.[1] Not very confident in his

---

[1] See the fine words of the 2nd Epistle attributed to Peter, iii. 13: καινοὺς οὐρανοὺς καὶ γῆν καινὴν προσδοκῶμεν ἐν οἷς δικαιοσύνη κατοικεῖ.

expectations of that eternity which makes resignation so easy to the Christian, he chides Jehovah, reproaches Him with His indolence, asks Him how He can leave the earth so long in the hands of the ungodly. As for himself, he does not doubt that the earth will one day be his own, and that his law will ensure the universal reign of justice and love.

It is the Jew who will win the day: to him belongs the future. Hope—what the Jew calls *tiqva*—this assurance of something which is by no means proved, but to which we attach ourselves all the more eagerly because we have no certainty of it—was the very soul of the Jew. His Psalms were like one continuous harp note, filling his life with harmony and melancholy faith: his prophets had the words of eternity: the second Isaiah, for instance, the prophet of the Captivity, depicted the future in the brightest colours that have ever been revealed to the dreams of man. The *Thora*, meanwhile, laid down the conditions of happiness (understand, of happiness here below) in the observance of the moral law, in the spirit of the family, in the love of duty.

I.

The establishment of the Jews in Rome dates from about sixty years B.C. They multiplied rapidly. Cicero represents resistance to them as an act of courage.[1] Cæsar favoured them, and found them faithful. The mob hated them, thought them malevolent, accused them of forming a secret society, the members of which unscrupulously sought their own advancement, to the injury of others. But these superficial judgments were not universal: the Jews had as many friends as detractors: men felt that there was something superior about them. The poor Jewish pedlar of the Trastevere often came home at night rich with alms from pious hands: women especially were drawn towards these ragged missionaries. Juvenal reckons among the vices with which he reproaches the ladies of his time, an inclination towards the Jewish religion.[2] The word of Zechariah[3] was verified to the letter; the world laid hold

---

[1] *Pro Flacco,* 28.   [2] Juv. *Sat.* vi. 546 et seq.
[3] Zech. viii. 23.

of the skirt of the Jew, and said to him, Lead us to Jerusalem.

The chief Jewish quarter lay beyond the Tiber;[1] that is to say, in the poorest and dirtiest part of the city,[2] probably not far from what is now the *Porta Portese*.[3] There, then as now, was the port of Rome, the place where the merchandize brought from Ostia

---

[1] Philo, *Leg. ad Caium*, § 23. Martial, i. xlii. (xxxv.) 3. The Jews continued to inhabit the Trastevere until the 15th and 16th century (Bosio, *Rom. Sott.* l. ii. ch. xxii. ; conf. *Corp. Inscr. Gr.* No. 9907). It is at the same time certain that under the Emperors they inhabited many other quarters of the city, and particularly the Campus Martius (*Corp.* Nos. 9905, 9906 ; Orelli, 2522 ; Garrucci, *Dissert. Arch.* ii. 163), outside the Porta Capena (Juv. *Sat.* iii. 11 et seq. ; Garrucci, *Cimitero*, p. 4), the island of the Tiber and the beggars' bridge (Juv. iv. 115, v. 8, xiv. 134; Martial, x. v. 3), and perhaps the Suburra (*Corp.* No. 6447).

[2] Martial, i. xlii. 3, vi. xciii. 4. Juv. *Sat.* xiv. 201 et seq.

[3] The principal Jewish cemetery of Rome was found in this neighbourhood by Bosio in 1602. Bosio, op. cit. ii. xxii. Aringhi, *Roma Sott.* i. ii. 23. Conf. *Corp. Inscr. Gr.* Nos. 9901 et seq., inscriptions found for the most part in the quarter. The trace of this catacomb is lost: F. Marchi searched for it in vain. Two other Jewish catacombs have since been found at Rome, on the Via Appia, near St. Sebastian. Garrucci, *Cimitero degli antichi Ebrei* (Roma, 1862); *Dissert. Arch.* ii. (Roma, 1866), 150 et seq. De Rossi, *Bull. di Arch. Crist.* 1867, 3, 16.

on lighters was unloaded. It was a quarter of Jews and Syrians, "nations born for servitude," as Cicero says.[1] The first nucleus of the Jewish population of Rome consisted of freedmen,[2] for the most part descendants of prisoners whom Pompey had carried thither. They had passed through a period of slavery without any change in their religious habits. An admirable thing in Judaism is that simplicity of faith, the result of which is that the Jew, transported a thousand leagues from his country, and after many generations, is a Jew still. The intercourse of the Roman synagogues with Jerusalem was constant.[3] The first colony had been reinforced by numerous emigrants.[4] These poor people landed by hundreds

---

[1] Provinc. cons. 5.

[2] Philo, *l.c.* Tacit. *Ann.* ii. 85. The inscriptions confirm this. Lévy, op. cit. p. 287. Conf. Mommsen, *Inscr. Regni Neap.* No. 6467 (*Captiva* is doubtful). De Rossi, *Bull.* 1864, 70, 92, 93. Conf. Acts vi. 9.

[3] Cicero, *Pro Flacco*, 28.

[4] Jos. *Ant.* xvii. iii. 5, xi. 1. Dio Cassius, xxxvii. 17. Tacit. *Ann.* ii. 85. Sueton. *Tib.* 36. Mommsen, *Inscr. Regni Neap.* No. 6467. There were in Rome at least four synagogues, two of which bore the names of Augustus and Agrippa (Herod

on the *Ripa*, and lived together in the Trastevere hard by, acting as porters, huckstering, bartering tapers for broken glass, and offering to the proud Italian population a type which at a later period must have become too familiar to them, that of the accomplished mendicant.[1] A Roman who respected himself never set foot in this abject quarter. It was a kind of "liberty" given up to despised classes and disgusting occupations; it was there that hides were tanned, that the entrails of animals were prepared for food, that rubbish of all kinds was put to rot.[2] So the poor creatures lived quietly enough in this forgotten corner, in the midst of bales of merchandize, of low public-houses, of the litter-carriers (Syri) who

---

Agrippa?). *Corp. Inscr. Gr.* 6447, 9902, 9903, 9904, 9905, 9906, 9907, 9909. Orelli, 2522. Garrucci, *Cimitero*, pp. 38—40; *Dissert. Arch.* ii. 161, 162, 163, 185. De Rossi, *Bull.* 1867, p. 16.

[1] Philo, *Leg. ad Caium*, § 23. Juv. iii. 14, 296, vi. 542. Mart. i. xlii. 3 et seq., x. iii. 3, 4, xii. lvii. 13, 14. Statius, *Silvæ*, i. vi. 72—74. The Jewish burial-places at Rome showed signs of great poverty. Bosio, *Roma Sott.* pp. 190 et seq. Lévy, *Epigraph. Beiträge zur Gesch. der Juden*, 283.

[2] Nardini, *Roma antica*, iii. 328—330 (4th ed.). Martial, vi. xciii. 4.

had their head-quarters there.¹ The police never came near them, unless their quarrels took place too often or ended in bloodshed. Few quarters of Rome were as free as this: politics never entered it. At ordinary times, not only was worship celebrated without interruption, but the work of conversion went on easily and quickly.²

Protected by the contempt which they inspired, and not very sensitive to the mockeries of more fashionable people, the Jews of the Trastevere thus lived a very active social and religious life. They had schools of *hakamim*:³ nowhere was the ritual and ceremonial part of the Law more scrupulously observed.⁴ The synagogues were more completely

---

¹ *Castra lecticariorum*, in the treatises *De regionibus urbis Romae*, regio xiv.; Canina, *Roma antica*, pp. 553, 554. Conf. Forcellini, s. v. *lecticarius*. The *Syrus* of the Latin comedies is usually a *lecticarius*.

² Josephus, *Ant.* xiv. x. 8; Acts xxviii. 31.

³ Conf. *Corp. Inscr. Gr.* No. 9908. Garrucci, *Cimitero*, pp. 57, 58.

⁴ Conf. Hor. *Sat.* i. ix. 69 et seq. Sueton. *Augustus*, 76. Seneca, *Epist.* xcv. 47. Persius, v. 179 et seq. Juvenal, xiv. 96 et seq. Martial, iv. iv. 6. The Jewish epigraphy of Rome bears witness to a population of a very precise ritual observance.

E

organized than any others which we know.¹ The titles "father and mother of the synagogue" were held in high esteem.² Rich female converts took Biblical names: they carried over their slaves to Judaism with them: they listened to expositions of Scripture by the doctors, built houses of prayer, and showed themselves proud of the consideration which they enjoyed in this little society.³ The poor Jew, as he asked an alms with trembling voice, found the opportunity of insinuating into the ear of the great

---

Lévy, *Epig. Beit.* pp. 285 et seq. Note the epithet φιλέντολος (*Corp.* No. 9904; Garrucci, *Dissert.* ii. 180, 185, 191, 192), answering to Ps. cxix. 48, and similar passages. Conf. Mommsen, *Inscr. Regni Neap.* No. 6467 (notwithstanding Garrucci, *Cim.* pp. 24, 25). The Jews carefully avoided the use of the letters D. M. on tombstones. They had also in Italy manufactures of lamps for their own use. (See Jewish lamp of the Parent Museum, found at Baiæ.)

[1] *Corp.* Nos. 9902 et seq. Garrucci, *Cim.* pp. 35 et seq., 67 et seq. *Diss. Arch.* ii. 161 et seq., 177, 181.

[2] *Corp.* Nos. 9904, 9905, 9908, 9909 (conf. Rénier, *Inscr. de l'Algerie*, No. 3340). Orelli, No. 2522 (conf. Gruter, p. 323, 3). Garrucci, *Cim.* pp. 52, 53.

[3] Orelli, 2522, 2523. Lévy, pp. 285, 311, 313. Garrucci, *Dissert. Arch.* ii. 166. Graetz, *Gesch. der Juden*, iv. 123, 506, 507.

Roman lady a word or two of the Law, and often gained the matron, who opened to him a hand full of small coin.[1] To keep the Sabbath and the Jewish festivals is, with Horace, a trait which marks a man of feeble mind—that is to say, puts him among the crowd: *unus multorum*.[2] Universal benevolence, the happiness of a last repose among the just, the assistance of the poor, purity of morals, the sweetness of the family life, the calm acceptance of the sleep of death —these are the sentiments which we find expressed in the Jewish, with the same peculiar accent of touching unction, of humility, of assured hope, as in the Christian inscriptions.[3] There were, indeed, Jews who were rich and powerful men of the world;

---

[1] Juvenal, vi. 542 et seq.   [2] Hor. *Sat.* i. ix. 71, 72.

[3] *Corp. Inscr. Gr.* 9904 et seq. Garrucci, *Cimitero*, pp. 31 et seq., 67 et seq., especially p. 68. *Dissert.* ii. 153 et seq. Notice particularly the beautiful expressions, φιλοπένης (Garrucci, *Dissert.* ii. 185; conf. Les Apôtres, p. 320, note 4), φιλόλαος (*Corp.* No. 9904. Garrucci, *Dissert.* p. 185; conf. 2 Macc. xv. 14), *concresconius, conlaboronius* (Garr. *Diss.* ii. 160, 161). The formulas of Jewish and Christian epigraphy are strangely analogous. It is true that the greater part of the Jewish inscriptions just quoted are much later than the reign of Claudius. But the spirit of the Jewish colony in Rome cannot have greatly changed.

such as Tiberius Alexander, who attained the greatest honours which the Empire had to give, more than once exercised a very important influence upon public affairs, and even, to the great annoyance of the Romans, had his statue in the Forum.[1] But such as he were no longer good Jews. The Herods, too, although ostentatiously observing their national rites at Rome,[2] were far from being genuine Israelites, if for no other reason, on account of their relations with pagans. The faithful poor looked upon these worldly brethren as renegades; as in our own day we may see Polish or Hungarian Jews treating with severity the Israelites in high places who forsake the synagogue, and bring up their children as Protestants, in the hope of thus liberating them from a contracted social circle.

A world of ideas was thus in motion upon the common quay where the merchandize of the whole earth was heaped up; but it was all lost to view in the

---

[1] M. Renier thinks that it is to Tiberius Alexander that Juvenal refers, i. 129—131, *arabarches* for *alabarches*. *Mém. de l'Acad. des Inscr.* Vol. xxvi. Pt. i. 294 et seq.

[2] Persius, v. 179 et seq. The allusion is to the *hanucca*.

tumult of a city as large as London and Paris.[1] We may be sure that the proud patricians who in their walks on the Aventine cast a glance on the other side of the Tiber, never suspected that the future was being made ready in that mass of hovels which lay at the foot of the Janiculum.[2] Near the port was a kind of lodging-house, well known to the people and the soldiers under the name of the *Taberna Meritoria*. There, to attract gazers, was shown what pretended to be a spring of oil flowing from the rock. From a very early date the Christians looked upon this spring of oil as symbolical: they alleged that its appearance had been simultaneous with the birth of Jesus.[3] At a later period the *Taberna* seems to have been turned into a church.[4] Under Alexander Severus, we find the Christians and the

---

[1] Platner and Bunsen, *Beschreibung der Stadt Rom.* i. 183, 185. The excavations recently made near the *agger* of Servius Tullius prove an almost incredibly large population.

[2] Conf. Tacit. *Hist.* v. 5.

[3] Orosius, vi. 18, 20. The lesser Christian Martyrology (ed. Rosweide), July 9. Vid. Forcellini, s. v. *meritorius*.

[4] According to Roman tradition, the Church of St. Maria in Trastevere has succeeded the *Taberna*. Vid. Nardini, *Roma antica*, iii. 336, 337. Platner and Bunsen, iii. Pt. iii. 659, 660.

innkeepers contending for the possession of a locality which had formerly been public, and which that excellent Emperor adjudged to the Christians.[1] We feel that we have here the birthplace of an old popular tradition of Christianity. Claudius, struck by "the progress of foreign superstitions," thought it an act of sound political conservatism to re-establish the haruspices. In a report made to the Senate, he complained of the indifference of the age to good discipline and the ancient usages of Italy. The Senate invited the Pontiffs to inquire which of the old practices it would be most advantageous to re-establish. All went well, and men believed that these respectable impostures were safe for all time to come.

It was natural that the capital should have heard the name of Christ some time before the intermediate countries were evangelized, as a high summit is lighted up when the valleys which lie between it and the sun are yet dark. Rome was

---

[1] Lampridius, *Vita Alex. Sever.* 49. Conf. Anastasius Bibl. *Vitæ Pontif. Rom.* xvii. (ed. Bianchini), taking note of the observations of Platner.

the meeting-place of all Oriental worships, the point upon the shores of the Mediterranean with which Syrians stood in the closest relation. They came thither in enormous numbers. Like all poor populations, who storm the walls of the great cities where they seek their fortune, they were humble and obliging. They all spoke Greek: the old Roman citizens, attached to the ancestral manners, were overwhelmed by this flood of foreigners, and lost ground every day.

We admit, then, that about the year 50 of our era, certain Syrian Jews, already converted to Christianity, entered the capital of the Empire, and communicated to the comrades whom they found there the faith which made them happy. No one in Rome that day suspected that the founder of a second Empire, another Romulus, was lying upon straw at the Port. Others soon followed: letters from Syria, brought by the new-comers, spoke of the movement as one that was constantly gaining strength. All these people smelt of garlic:[1] these ancestors of Roman prelates were poor, dirty *proletaires*, without

---

[1] Fœtentes Judæi. Amm. Marc. xxii. 5.

distinction, without manners, clad in filthy gaberdines, having the bad breath of men whose food is insufficient. Their haunts exhaled that odour of wretchedness which arises from human beings who are coarsely clothed, badly fed, closely crowded.[1] We know the names of the two Jews who had most to do with this movement. They were a pious couple, Aquila, a Jew of Pontus, practising the same handicraft of tent-making as Paul, and Priscilla his wife. Driven from Rome, they took refuge at Corinth, where they soon became the intimate friends and zealous fellow-workers of St. Paul. Aquila and Priscilla are thus the two oldest members of the Church of Rome known to us. There they are hardly remembered.[2] Legend, always unjust, because always moulded by reasons of policy, has expelled from the Christian Pantheon these two obscure

---

[1] Juvenal, iii. 14. Mart. iv. iv. 7.

[2] The attribution of the ancient ".title of St. Prisca" on the Aventine to Priscilla, wife of Aquila, is the result of a mistake. Vid. De Rossi (*Bull. di Arch. Crist.* 1867, 44 et seq.), who is unable to trace the identification further back than the eighth century.

artizans, to award the honour of founding the Church of Rome to a name more fully answering to its proud pretensions. We, however, may discern the true starting-point of Western Christianity, not in the pompous basilica which has been dedicated to St. Peter, but in the ancient *ghetto* of the Porta Portese. It is the trace of these poor wandering Jews, bringing with them from Syria the religion of the world, these labouring men, dreaming in their wretchedness of the kingdom of God, that we must try to recover. We do not deny to Rome her essential pre-eminence: she was probably the first city of the Western world, and even of Europe, where Christianity established itself. But in place of those proud basilicas, with their insolent motto, *Christus vincit, Christus regnat, Christus imperat,* she would do well to build a humble chapel in memory of the two good Jews who first uttered upon her quays the name of Jesus.

In any case, a fact of capital importance which we must notice at this stage of our inquiry is, that the Church of Rome was not, like the Churches of Asia Minor, of Macedonia and of Greece, a Pauline foundation. It was a Jewish-Christian product, attaching itself directly to the Church of Jerusalem.[1] In it, Paul will never be on his own ground: he will feel the presence in this great Church of many weaknesses, which he will treat with indulgence, but which will offend his lofty idealism.[2] Given to circumcision and to external observances;[3] Ebionite[4] both in its love of abstinences[5] and in its doctrine; more Jewish than Christian in its conception of the person and death of Jesus;[6] strongly attached to millenarianism,[7]—the Roman Church displays from

---

[1] Acts xviii. 2. Commentary (of the deacon Hilary) on the Epp. of St. Paul, at the end of the Works of St. Ambrose, Benedict. Ed. Vol. ii. Pt. ii. (Paris, 1686), col. 25, 30. This Commentary is the production of a writer well acquainted with the traditions of the Roman Church.

[2] Rom. xiv. xv. 1—13.

[3] Rom. xiv. xv. 8. Conf. Tacit. *Hist.* v. 5.

[4] Epiphan. *Hær.* xxx. 18. Conf. xxx. 2, 15, 16, 17.

[5] Rom. xiv. Pseudo-Clem. Hom. xiv. 1.

[6] Commentary of Hilary, cited above, *ibid.* Conf. the assertion of Artemo in Eusebius, *H. E.* v. 28. Pseudo-Clem. Hom. (a work of Roman origin) xvi. 14 et seq.

[7] This is the reason why the Judeo-Christian and millenarian literature has been more fully preserved in Latin than in Greek (4th Book of Esdras, Leptogenesis, Assumption of Moses). The Greek fathers of the 4th and 5th centuries were very hostile to

the beginning the essential characteristics which distinguished it throughout its long and marvellous history. The legitimate daughter of Jerusalem, the Roman Church will always have a certain ascetic and sacerdotal character, opposed to the Protestant tendency of Paul. Peter will be her real head: afterwards, as the political and hierarchical spirit of old Rome penetrates her, she will truly become the New Jerusalem—the city of the Pontificate, of a hieratic and solemn religion, of material sacraments alone sufficient for justification—the city of ascetics after the manner of James Obliam, with his hardened knees and the plate of gold on his forehead. She will be the Church of authority. If we are to believe

---

this literature, even to the Apocalypse. The Greek Church depends more directly upon Paul than the Latin: in the East, Paul actually destroyed his enemies. Note the favourable reception which Montanism (a heresy which had elements in common with Jewish Christianity), and other sects of the same kind, met with in Rome. Tertullian, *Adv. Prax.* 1. St. Hippolytus (?) Philosophum. ix. 7, 12, 13 et seq. Especially vid. in Eusebius, *II. E.* all that relates to the heresy of Artemo and Theodotus, and note the principle of the Artemonites, according to which the traditional doctrine of the Church of Rome had been altered after the time of Zephyrinus.

her, the only satisfactory evidence of an apostolical mission will be to show a letter signed by apostles, and to produce a certificate of orthodoxy.[1] The good and the evil which the Church of Jerusalem did to a nascent Christianity, the Church of Rome will do to the universal Church. In vain Paul will address to her his noble Epistle, expounding the mystery of the Cross of Christ and salvation by faith alone. She will hardly understand it. But Luther, fourteen centuries and a half later, will understand it, and will open a new era in the secular series of the alternate triumphs of Peter and of Paul.

II.

An event of capital importance in the history of the world took place in the year 61. Paul, a prisoner, was taken to Rome, there to prosecute the appeal which he had made to the tribunal of the Emperor. A sort of profound instinct had always made Paul long to take this journey. His arrival in Rome was an event in his life almost as decisive as

---

[1] Vid. the Pseudo-Clementine Homilies (a Roman work), particularly Hom. xvii.

his conversion. In it he believed himself to have attained the highest point of his apostolical career, and doubtless remembered the dream in which, after one of his days of struggle, Christ had appeared to him and said, "Be of good cheer, Paul; for as thou hast testified of me in Jerusalem, so must thou bear witness also at Rome."[1]

You are not ignorant of the profound divisions which, in this first age of the foundation of Christianity, parted the disciples of Jesus—divisions so profound, that none of the differences which now separate the orthodox from the heretics and schismatics of the whole world, are to be compared with the disagreement between Peter and Paul. The Church of Jerusalem, obstinately attached to Judaism, refused all communion to the uncircumcised, no matter how devout they might be. Paul, on the contrary, declared that to maintain the old law was to do a wrong to Jesus, inasmuch as it was equivalent to supposing that, over and above his merits, something else could contribute to the justification of the faith-

---

[1] Acts xix. 21, xxiii. 11.

ful. However strange it may appear, it is certain that the Jewish Christians of Jerusalem, with James at their head, organized active missions to counteract the effect of those of Paul, and that the emissaries of these ardent conservatives followed in some sort upon the track of the Apostle of the Gentiles. Peter belonged to the party of Jerusalem, to which he contributed that kind of timid moderation which appears to have been the basis of his character.[1] Did Peter also come to Rome? Once, this question was one of the most burning that could be raised. Formerly, religious history was only a department of theology, and written, not to narrate, but to prove. In the great rebellion, animated by so much courageous and ardent conviction, which in the sixteenth century roused half Europe against the court of Rome, men gradually elevated the denial of Peter's residence at Rome into a kind of dogma. The Bishop of Rome is the successor of St. Peter, said the Catho-

---

[1] The rivalry of Peter and Paul is the capital discovery of Christian Baur and the Tübingen school; but these ingenious critics have not only gravely overstated their thesis, but have weakened it by the adduction of arguments which have really nothing to do with the question.

lics, and as such the head of Christendom. What more efficacious way of refuting this reasoning than by maintaining that Peter never set foot in Rome? For ourselves, we may approach the question with the most perfect impartiality. We have not the slightest belief that Jesus intended to set a chief of any kind over his Church. To begin at the beginning, it is doubtful whether the idea of the Church, as it was developed at a later time, ever existed in the mind of the Founder of Christianity. The word *ecclesia* occurs only in the Gospel of Matthew. What, at all events, is quite certain is, that the idea of the *episcopos*, in the form which it took in the second century, was no part of the thought of Jesus. It is himself who, during his brief Galilean apparition, is the living *episcopos:* afterwards the Spirit will inspire each individual soul until the Master's return. Even if any idea of an *ecclesia* and an *episcopos* can be ascribed to Jesus, it is absolutely indubitable that he never dreamed of the future *episcopos* of the city of Rome, that impious city, that centre of all the earth's impurity, of whose existence he was possibly hardly aware, and which he must have looked upon in the same sombre light as did all other Jews. If there is anything in the world which Jesus did not institute, it is the Papacy; that is, the idea that the Church is a monarchy. We may, then, discuss the question of Peter's coming to Rome entirely at our ease: the answer fastens upon us no dogmatic consequences: nor from it, whatever it may be, shall we be able to infer that Leo XIII. either is or is not supreme over Christian consciences. Whether Peter was at Rome or not, is a matter which has neither moral nor political interest for us. It is a curious historical question, and we must not seek to import any other significance into it.

Let us say, in the first place, that the unfortunate chronological scheme which, according to Catholics, brings Peter to Rome in the year 42, and makes the duration of his Pontificate twenty-two or twenty-three years,—a scheme borrowed from Eusebius and Jerome,—is open to the most decisive objections. Nothing can be less admissible. To remove all doubt on the subject, it is only necessary to recollect that the persecution which Peter suffered at Jerusalem at the hands of Herod Agrippa I. took place in the very year in which that monarch died, namely, in 44.[1] It would be a work of supererogation to controvert at length a theory which cannot now boast a single rational advocate. We may indeed go further, and affirm that Peter had not yet arrived in Rome when Paul was brought there, that is to say, in the year 61. The Epistle of Paul to the Romans, written about the year 58, or which could not have been written, at most, more than two years and a half before Paul's arrival at Rome, is an important branch of the evidence; it is impossible to imagine that St. Paul could have written to the disciples, of whom Peter was the head, without making the least mention of him. The last chapter of the Acts of the Apostles is still more decisive. This chapter, and especially verses 17 to 29, are unintelligible if Peter was at Rome when Paul came there. We may take it, then, as absolutely certain that Peter did not come to Rome before Paul, that is to say, before the year 61, as nearly as we can fix it.

But did he come to Rome after Paul? This is

---

[1] Acts xii. Jos. *Ant.* xix. viii. 2.

what no one has yet been able to prove. Not only is there no impossibility in this later journey of Peter to Rome, but strong reasons militate in its favour. Besides the evidence of the Fathers of the second and third century, which is not without weight, three arguments, the force of which appears to me to be not contemptible, may be adduced on that side.

1. It cannot be denied that Peter died a martyr's death. The evidence of the fourth Gospel, of Clement of Rome, of the fragment which is called the Canon of Muratori, of Dionysius of Corinth, of Caius, of Tertullian, leaves no room for doubt.[1] Even if

---

[1] John xxi. 18, 19, compared with xii. 32, 33, xiii. 36, passages on any hypothesis written before the year 150, and the more decisive in that they are indirect, and suppose the fact in question to be universally known. 2 Peter i. 14. Canon of Muratori, 1. 36, 37. Clem. Rom. *Ad. Cor.* i. ch. 5. Dionysius of Corinth and Caius, priest of Rome, quoted by Eusebius, *H. E.* ii. 25. Tertull. *Præsc.* 36; *Adv. Marc.* iv. 5; *Scorpiace*, 15. Luke xxii. 32, 33, compared with the passage in the Canon of Muratori previously quoted, and with John xiii. 36—38, furnishes much matter for reflection. Conf. Macarius Magnes, bk. iv. § 4 (still unedited). Rev. xviii. 20 is also strongly on the side of the text.

the fourth Gospel be apocryphal, even if the twenty-first chapter were added to it at a later date, it does not alter the case. It is clear that, in the passage in which Jesus announces to Peter that he will die the same death as himself, we have the expression of an opinion strongly held in the Church about the year 120 or 130, and to which allusion was made as to a thing which everybody knew. Now it is not to be supposed that St. Peter suffered martyrdom elsewhere than in Rome. Indeed, it was only in Rome that the persecution of Nero was violent. The martyrdom of Peter at Jerusalem or at Antioch is much less explicable.

2. Our second argument is drawn from the first Epistle attributed to Peter, v. 13. Babylon in this passage is plainly Rome. If the Epistle is authentic, the passage is decisive. If it is apocryphal, the inference which we may draw from it is not less convincing. The author, whoever he may be, wishes to make his readers believe that the work in question is the work of Peter. Consequently, to give probability to his forgery, he deals with local circumstances in a way accordant with

what he knew, and with what men at that time believed that they knew, of the life of Peter. If, in such a frame of mind, he has dated the letter from Rome, it means that, when it was written, the received opinion was that Peter had lived at Rome. On any hypothesis, the first Epistle of Peter is a work of great antiquity, which very soon attained a position of high authority in the Church.

3. The scheme which lies at the basis of the Ebionite Acts of St. Peter is also well worth consideration. This scheme shows us St. Peter everywhere following Simon the Magician (by whom we are to understand St. Paul), with a view of contending against his false doctrines. M. Lipsius[1] has applied an admirable critical sagacity to the analysis of this curious legend. He has shown that the foundation of the different editions which have come down to us was a primitive narrative, written about the year 130, a narrative which brings Peter to Rome in order that he may overcome Simon Paul at the very centre

---

[1] *Römische Petrussage*, pp. 13 et seq., especially pp. 16, 18, 41, 42. Conf. *Recogn.* i. 74, iii. 65. Apocryphal letter of Clement to James at the beginning of the Homilies, ch. i.

of his influence, and, after having brought to confusion this father of all error, may die there. It seems difficult to suppose that the Ebionite author, at so early a date, would have made Peter's journey to Rome of so much importance, if that journey had had no foundation in fact. The scheme of the Ebionite legend must, in spite of the fables which are mixed up with it, have had a basis of reality. It is quite possible that St. Peter may have come to Rome, as he came to Antioch, in the track of Paul, and in part with a view of neutralizing his influence. The Christian community about the year 60 was in a state of mind very unlike the quiet expectation of the twenty years which followed the death of Jesus. The missions of Paul, and the ease with which the Jews made their journeys, had brought distant expeditions into fashion. The apostle Philip is indicated by an old and persistent tradition as having gone to settle at Hierapolis, in Asia Minor.

I therefore look upon the tradition of Peter's residence in Rome as probably true; but I believe that it was of short duration, and that the apostle suffered martyrdom soon after his arrival in the Eternal City.

III.

You are not ignorant of the mystery which enshrouds those events of the primitive history of Christianity which we would willingly know in exactest outline. The deaths of the apostles Peter and Paul are covered by a veil which will never be penetrated. The most probable supposition is that both disappeared in the great massacre of the Christians which was ordered by Nero. As to this last fact, the doubt which so often attends our investigations into the origins of Christianity is absolutely impossible, for the monstrous story is told us by Tacitus, in a passage the authenticity of which cannot be disputed.

On the 19th of July, in the year 64, a fire of extraordinary violence broke out in Rome.[1] It began near the Porta Capena, in the part of the Circus

---

[1] Tacitus, *Ann.* xv. 38—44, 52. Sueton. *Nero*, 31, 38, 39; *Vesp.* 8. Dio Cassius, lxii. 16—18. Plin. *Hist. Nat.* xvii. 1 (1). Euseb. *Chron.* ad ann. 65. Orelli, *Inser.* No. 736, which appears quite authentic. Sulpicius Severus (ii. 29) copies Tacitus almost word for word. Orosius (vii. 7) for the most part follows Suetonius.

Maximus contiguous to the Palatine and the Cœlian Hills. This quarter of the city contained many shops, full of inflammable materials, whence the flames spread with frightful rapidity. From this point the fire made the round of the Palatine, ravaged the Velabrum, the Forum, the Carinæ, mounted the hills, committed great damage on the Palatine, redescended into the valleys, devouring for six days and seven nights closely compact quarters, pierced by tortuous streets. An enormous pulling down of houses, which was effected at the foot of the Esquiline, stopped it for awhile; but it burned up again, and lasted three days longer. The number of deaths was considerable. Of the fourteen "regions" into which the city was divided, three were wholly destroyed, seven others reduced to blackened walls. Rome was a city singularly closely built and very densely peopled. The disaster was frightful, and such as men had never known the like.

Nero was at Antium when the fire broke out. He did not return to the city until the moment at which the conflagration was drawing near to his "domus transitoria." It was impossible to save anything from the flames. The imperial palaces of the Palatine, the "domus transitoria" itself, with its dependencies, all the surrounding quarter, were overwhelmed. Nero plainly did not make any great effort to save his mansion. The sublime horror of the spectacle carried him out of himself. At a later period, men said that he had watched the flames from the height of a tower, and that there, clad in theatrical attire and with a lyre in his hand, he had sung, in the pathetic metre of the ancient elegy, the ruin of Ilium.[1]

---

[1] The account of Tacitus (*Ann.* xv. 39) does not mention this circumstance. Tacitus, it is true, speaks of a report that Nero, during the fire, sang the ruin of Troy "in his private theatre." If this was so, it could only be at Antium, which would be very awkward. It is plain that Tacitus mentions the report without adopting it. The accounts of Suetonius and of Dion do not agree as to details: one places the scene at the Esquiline, the other at the Palatine. The anecdote no doubt arose from the poem entitled *Troica* which Nero composed and read in public the year after the fire, and which could be understood in a double sense, like the poem of Lucan, "*Catacausmus Iliacus*," written about the same time. Dio. Cass. lxii. 29. Servius ad Virg. *Georg.* iii. 36. *Æn.* v. 370. Persius, i. 123. Stat. *Silv.* ii. vii. 58—61. Juvenal, viii. 221. Petron. p. 105 (ed. Bücheler). The impropriety of such allusions struck everybody, and gave rise to the phrase that Nero "had played the lyre upon the ruins of his country." (The expression

This was a legend, the product of time and successive exaggerations. But a matter upon which all were agreed from the first was, that Nero had ordered the fire, or at least had rekindled it when it was about to die out. It was believed that persons belonging to his household had been seen setting fire to buildings on all sides. In certain places, it was said, the flames had been kindled by men pretending to be drunk. The conflagration seemed as if it had begun at the same moment in more quarters than one. Men told the tale that, during the fire, soldiers and watchmen, whose business it was to put it out, had been seen to stir it up, and to thwart the

---

patriæ ruinis is in Tacit. *Ann.* xv. 42.) This phrase became an anecdote; and as legend is usually born of an apt word, a true sentiment, changed into a reality by help of violence done to time and space, the poem *Troica* was put back to the actual date of the catastrophe. The anecdote offered an almost insurmountable difficulty to those who, like Tacitus, knew that when the fire broke out Nero was at Antium; and to make their story less inconsistent with fact, they supposed that he had sung his elegy " on a private stage." Those who did not know that, for the greater part of the time that the fire lasted, Nero was at Antium, transported the scene of the anecdote to Rome, where each chose for it the most theatrical *locale* that he could find. The pretended *Torre di Nerone* that is now shown belongs to the middle ages.

efforts which were made to extinguish it; and all this with an air of menace, as persons who were obeying superior commands.[1] Massive constructions of stone, close to the imperial residence, the site of which Nero was known to covet, were knocked to pieces as in a siege. When the conflagration began for the second time, it was in buildings belonging to Tigellinus. What confirmed suspicion was, that after the fire, Nero, under pretext of removing the ruins at his own expense, in order that the sites might be left free to their owners, undertook the task of carrying away the building materials, and allowed no one to come near as he executed it. Things were much worse when he was seen to grasp his own advantage among the ruins of the city, and his new palace, that Golden House which had so long been the plaything of his delirious imagination, rose upon the site of the old temporary residence, enlarged by the area which the fire had cleared.[2] Men thought that his object had been to prepare the site of this new

---

[1] It is possible that these were malefactors, increasing the disorder for purposes of plunder.

[2] Sueton. *Nero*, 31, 38.

palace, to justify a long-meditated reconstruction, to procure funds by the appropriation of whatever was left by the fire; in a word, to satisfy the foolish vanity which would willingly have had Rome to rebuild, that it might henceforth date from his reign and be known as Neropolis.

Every respectable inhabitant of the city was outraged. The most precious antiquities of Rome, the houses of old captains still decorated with triumphal spoils, the holiest objects, the trophies, the ancient *ex votos*, the most venerated temples, all that belonged to the ancestral Roman worship, had disappeared. There was an universal mourning for the recollections and the legends of the land. It was in vain that Nero undertook at his own cost to relieve the misery which he had caused: it was in vain that he pointed out that all that had been done really amounted to no more than a clearing and a cleansing, and that the new city would be far superior to the old: no true Roman would believe him: all, to whom a city was something more than a mere heap of stones, were wounded to the heart: the conscience of the country was hurt. This temple, built by

Evander, this, by Servius Tullius: the sacred enclosure of Jupiter Stator, the palace of Numa: these *penates* of the Roman people, these monuments of so many victories, these masterpieces of Greek art,— how could their loss be repaired? In comparison with them, what was the worth of these ostentatious splendours, these vast monumental perspectives, these straight lines without end? Ceremonies of expiation were gone through: the Sibylline books were consulted: the women especially celebrated various *piacula*. But there remained the secret feeling that a crime, an infamy, had been committed.

An infernal idea then suggested itself to Nero's mind. He looked to see if there were not somewhere in the world wretches whom the citizens of Rome hated still more bitterly than himself, and upon whom he could divert the odium of the fire. He thought of the Christians. The horror which they showed for the temples and buildings most venerated by the Romans, rendered it a plausible idea that they had been the authors of a fire, one effect of which had been to destroy these sanctuaries. Their gloomy air in presence of the monuments was like an insult to the land. Rome was a highly religious city, in which any one who protested against the national worship was soon conspicuous. We must remember that some rigid Jews went so far as to be unwilling to touch any coin which bore an effigy, and thought it as great a crime to look at or to carry an image as to carve one. Others refused to pass through a gate of the city which was surmounted by a statue. All this kind of thing excited the people's mockery and ill-will. Possibly the talk of the Christians about the great final conflagration,[1] their sinister prophecies, their way of repeating that the world was soon coming to an end, and that by fire, contributed to fix upon them the character of incendiaries. It may even be surmised that some of the faithful had committed imprudences, and that there was a pretext for accusing them of wishing to justify their oracles at any cost, by preparing an earthly prelude to the fires of heaven.

In four years and a half more, the Apocalypse

---

[1] Conf. *Carmina Sibyllina*, iv. 172 et seq. (a passage written about the year 75); also 2 Pet. iii. 7—13.

will celebrate in song a burning of Rome, to which in all probability the event of 64 will furnish more than one circumstance. The destruction of Rome by fire was indeed a dream of both Jews and Christians; but it was no more than a dream: it was enough for those pious sectaries to behold in spirit saints and angels applauding from the height of heaven what they regarded as a just expiation.[1]

The first step taken was to arrest a certain number of persons who were suspected of belonging to the new sect, and to crowd them together in an imprisonment[2] which was itself a severe punishment.[3] They confessed their faith,—a confession that might be looked upon as also a confession of the crime judged to be inseparable from it. These first arrests were followed by many others.[4] The majority of the accused appear to have been proselytes, who observed the precepts and agreements of the treaty

---

[1] Rev. xviii.

[2] συνηθροίσθη, Clem. Rom. *Ad Cor.* i. 6.

[3] Shepherd of Hermas, i. vis. iii. 2.

[4] *Multitudo ingens*, Tacit. *Ann.* xv. 44. πολὺ πλῆθος ἐκλεκτῶν, Clem. Rom. *Ad Cor.* i. 6. ὄχλος πολύς, Rev. vii. 9, 14.

of Jerusalem.[1] It is not to be supposed that any true Christians informed against their brethren; but papers may have been seized; neophytes, hardly yet fully initiated, may have been weak under torture. Men were surprised at the number of adherents which these obscure doctrines had gained, and spoke of the fact almost with terror. But all sensible people found the evidence which connected the Christians with the fire extremely weak. Their true crime, it was said, was hatred of the human race. However convinced that the conflagration was the work of Nero, many grave Romans saw in this cast of the police net a means of freeing the city from a deadly pest. Tacitus, notwithstanding some gleam of pity, is of this opinion.[2] As to Suetonius, he counts among the praiseworthy actions of Nero the punishments which he inflicted on the adherents of the new and maleficent superstition.[3]

The punishments were frightful. Such refinements of cruelty had never before been seen. Almost

---

[1] Rev. xii. 17, which appears to be an allusion to the atrocities of the year 64.

[2] *Ann.* xv. 44.   [3] *Nero*, 16.

all the Christians who had been arrested were *humiliores*, persons of no condition. The punishment of these miserable creatures, whose crime was high treason or sacrilege, was to be delivered to wild beasts, or to be burned alive in the amphitheatre,[1] with the addition of cruel scourgings.[2] One of the most hideous features of Roman manners was to make a festival of public executions, a spectacle of butchery.[3] The amphitheatres[4] were turned into places of execution: the tribunals furnished forth the arena. The criminals of the whole world were

---

[1] Paul, *Sentent.* v. xxix. 1, "Humiliores bestiis objiciuntur vel vivi exuruntur: honestiores capite puniuntur." Ulpian, *Digest.* l. 6, pr., *ad legem Juliam peculatus* (xlviii. 13). Conf. θεατριζόμενοι, Heb. x. 33; Jos. *B.J.* vii. iii. 1. Letter of the churches of Vienne and Lyons in Euseb. *H.E.* v. 1. *Mart. Polyc.* 2, 3, 4, 11—13. Tertull. *Apol.* 12, 40. Lactant. *De mortibus Persecut.* 13, 21. Death in the circus was the punishment of criminal slaves. Petron. pp. 145, 146 (ed. Bücheler).

[2] Herm. *Pastor,* i. vis. iii. 2. Conf. the Acts of the Martyrs of Lyons (Eus. *H.E.* v. 1, 36) and of Africa, § 18 (Ruinart, p. 100).

[3] Philo, *In Flaccum,* § 10. Jos. *B.J.* viii. iii. 1. Sueton. *Nero,* 12.

[4] The amphitheatres of this age were of wood. Their construction in stone dates from the Flavian Emperors. Sueton. *Vesp.* 9.

brought to Rome for the supply of the circus and the amusement of the people.[1]

To the cruelty of punishment, on this occasion was added derision. The victims were reserved for a festival, to which, beyond doubt, an expiatory character was given. The *ludus matutinus*, consecrated to the combats of wild animals,[2] saw a procession without precedent. Criminals, covered with the skins of beasts, were thrown into the arena, and there torn to pieces by dogs; others were crucified;[3] others, clad in garments saturated with oil or pitch or resin, were fastened to gibbets and reserved to illuminate the festival of the night. When the day declined, these living flambeaux were lighted. Nero lent for the show his magnificent gardens beyond the

---

[1] *Martyrium S. Ignatii*, 2, εἰς τέρψιν τοῦ δήμου.

[2] Seneca, *Epist*. 7. Sueton. *Claud*. 34. Martial, x. xxv. xiii. xcv. Tertull. *Apol*. 15. Conf. Ovid, *Metam*. xi. 26. Virgil (*redeunt spectacula mane*). Orelli, Nos. 2553, 2554. The martyrs of Carthage (§ 17) took their last meal at night.

[3] The reading *aut flammandi atque* gives room for doubt (vid. Bernays, *Ueber die Chronik des Sulp. Sev.* pp. 54, 55, note), but without important results. Perhaps the second *aut* is superfluous. *Flammandi*, in the sense of *ut flammarentur*, is right.

Tiber, on the site of what is now the Borgo, the Piazza and Basilica of St. Peter.[1] Here was a circus, begun by Caligula and continued by Claudius. The central point of the *spina* was marked by an obelisk brought from Heliopolis—that which now rises in the centre of the Piazza of St. Peter's.[2] This spot had already witnessed massacres by torch-light. Caligula, as he took his walks, had there caused to be beheaded by night a certain number of consular personages, senators and Roman ladies.[3] The idea of substituting for torches human bodies impregnated with inflammable substances, might appear ingenious. As a punishment, this method of burning alive was not new: what was called the *tunica molesta*[4] was the ordinary

---

[1] The "pré Noiron" of the middle ages.

[2] Sueton. *Claud.* 21. Tacit. *Ann.* xiv. 14. Pliny, *Hist. Nat.* xv. xl. (76), xxxvi. xi. (15). This circus was the *naumachia*, spoken of in the Acts of Peter. Conf. Platner and Bunsen, *Beschreibung der Stadt Rom.* ii. i. 39. The obelisk was removed by Sixtus V. It was formerly in the Sacristy of St. Peter's.

[3] Senec. *De Ira*, iii. 18.

[4] Juvenal, *Sat.* i. 155, 156, viii. 233—235. Martial, *Epigr.* x. xxv. 5. Conf. Seneca, *De Ira*, iii. 3. Notice the *uri* of the gladiators' engagement. Hor. *Sat.* ii. vii. 58. Petron. p. 149 (ed. Bücheler). Seneca, *Epist.* 37.

penalty of arson: but it had never before been made a method of artificial illumination. By the light of these hideous torches, Nero, who had brought night races into fashion,[1] showed himself in the arena, sometimes in his jockey's dress mingling with the people, sometimes driving his chariot and bidding for applause. Signs of public compassion were, however, not wholly wanting. Even those who thought the Christians guilty, and openly declared that they deserved condign punishment, held these cruel pleasures in horror. Wise men would have done no more than public utility demanded. They would have purged the city of dangerous characters, while avoiding the appearance of sacrificing so many criminals to the ferocity of a single man.[2]

---

[1] Sueton. *Nero*, 35.

[2] Tacit. *Ann.* xv. 44. Sueton. *Nero*, 16. Clem. Rom. *Ad Cor.* 1. 6. Tertull. *Apol.* 5 (he appeals to the official *commentarii*); *Ad Nat.* 1. 7. *Scorpiace*, 15. Euseb. *H.E.* ii. 22, 25. *Chron.* ad ann. 13 Ner. Lactant. *De Mortibus Persecut.* 2. Sulp. Sev. *Hist. Sacra*, ii. 29. Oros. vii. 7. Gregory of Tours, i. 24. Georg. Syncell. *Chron.* p. 339. The echo of this persecution and allusions to the tortures suffered by the Christians are to be found in

Women, virgins, were involved in these horrible games.[1] The nameless indignities which they suffered formed part of the festival. Under Nero, a custom had grown up of compelling criminals in the amphitheatre to play mythological parts, ending in the death of the actors. These hideous operas, in which mechanical science was applied to produce prodigious effects,[2] were a novelty. The unfortunate one was brought into the arena, richly clad as the god or hero who was devoted to death, and there represented, in the circumstances of his punishment, some tragical scene of the fables

---

Rev. vi. 9 et seq., vii. 9 et seq., xii. 10—12 and even 17, xiii. 7, 10, 15, 16, xiv. 12, 13, xvi. 6, xvii. 6, xviii. 24, xx. 4; Heb. x. 32 et seq.; Herm. *Pastor*, i. vis. iii. c. 2; *Carm. Sibyll.* iv. 136, v. 136 et seq., 385 et seq.; possibly in Matt. xxiv. 9 (θλίψις). We shall show presently that the Apocalypse directly arose out of the persecution of Nero. The inscription relating to this persecution (Orelli, No. 730) is a forgery.

[1] Clem. Rom. *Ad Cor.* i. 6. Διὰ ζῆλον διωχθεῖσαι γυναῖκες Δαναΐδες καὶ Δίρκαι, αἰκίσματα δεινὰ καὶ ἀνόσια παθοῦσαι ἐπὶ τὸν τῆς πίστεως βέβαιον δρόμον κατήντησαν, καὶ ἔλαβον γέρας γενναῖον αἱ ἀσθενεῖς τῷ σώματι.

[2] Martial, *Spectac.* xxi.

consecrated by sculptors and by poets.¹ Sometimes it was Hercules Furens, burning upon Mount Œta, and tearing from his skin the shirt of burning pitch; sometimes, Orpheus torn in pieces by a bear, Dædalus falling from heaven and devoured by wild beasts, Pasiphaé suffering the embraces of the bull, Attys mutilated;² sometimes there were horrible masquerades, in which the men were accoutred as priests of Saturn, with the red cloak upon their backs—the women, as priestesses of Ceres, wearing fillets on their foreheads;³ and again, dramatic pieces, in the course of which the hero was actually put to death, as, for instance, Laureolus, or representations of tragic actions, such as that of Mucius Scævola.⁴ At the conclusion, Mercury, with a rod of iron reddened

---

[1] Martial, *Spectac.* v. (conf. Sueton. *Nero*, 12; Apuleius, *Metam.* i. 10), viii. (conf. Sueton. *l.c.*), xxi. Tertullian, *Apol.* 15 (conf. 9). *Ad nationes*, i. 10. The *tunica molesta* usually implied the representation of Hercules upon Mount Œta (Juven. viii. 235; Martial, x. xxv. 5).

[2] Perhaps he was confounded with Adonis, killed by the wild boar.

[3] Acts of the Martyrs of Africa, § 18.

[4] Martial, *Epigr.* viii. xxx., x. xxv.

in the fire, touched each corpse for the purpose of detecting any sign of life; while masked attendants, representing Pluto or Orcas, dragged off the dead by the feet, killing with mallets those that still quivered.[1]

The most respectable Christian ladies were compelled to bear a part in these horrors. Some played the part of the Danaids, others that of Dirce.[2] It is difficult to see how the tale of the Danaids could furnish materials for a sanguinary spectacle. The punishment which all mythological tradition assigns to those guilty women, and in the endurance of which they were exhibited,[3] was not sufficiently cruel to minister to the pleasures of Nero and the habitual spectators of his amphitheatre. Perhaps they passed in procession, carrying their urns,[4] and received the fatal blow from an actor who represented Lynceus.[5] Perhaps Amymone, one of their number,

---

[1] Tertull. *Apol.* 15. Conf. Sueton. *Nero*, 36.

[2] Clem. Rom. *Ad Cor.* i. 6. Vid. the notes of Hefele.

[3] Pausanias, x. xxxi. 9, 11. *Museo Pio-Clem.* iv. plate 36.

[4] *Museo Pio-Clem.* ii. 2. Guigniaut, *Rel. de l'Ant.* pl. No. 606 a. Conf. *Bulletino dell. Inst. di corr. Arch.* 1848, 119—123.

[5] Schol. on Euripides, *Hecuba*, 886. Conf. Servius ad Virg. *Æn.* x. 497.

was exhibited as pursued by a satyr, and violated by Neptune.[1] Possibly these poor creatures went through the whole series of the punishments of Tartarus under the eyes of the audience, and died at last after hours of torture. Representations of hell were the fashion. Some years earlier, certain Egyptians and Nubians had been very successful in Rome in giving exhibitions by night, in which were shown in due order the horrors of the under-world,[2] as displayed in the pictures of the royal tombs at Thebes, and especially in that of Sethi I.

As to the punishment of the Dirces, there is no doubt whatever. Every one knows the colossal group called the Farnese Bull, now in the Museum of Naples. Amphion and Zethus are binding Dirce to the horns of an untamed bull, which is about to drag her over the rocks and the briars of Cithæron.[3]

---

[1] Hygin. *Fabulæ*, 169. Conf. for what follows, 179.

[2] Sueton. *Caius*, 57.

[3] *Real Museo Borbonico*, xiv. pl. iv. v. Guignaut, *Rel. de l'Ant.* pl. 728, 728a. Gargiulo, i. Nos. 1—3, iii. No. 23. Conf. *Memorie della R. Accademia Ercolanese*, iii. 386 et seq., iv. Pt. i, vii. 1 et seq. Raoul-Rochette, *Choix de Peint. de Pompéi*, pL xxiii. 277—288. *Ann. de l'Institut de corr. Arch.* xi. (1839),

This indifferent work of Rhodian sculpture, transported to Rome about the time of Augustus, was the object of universal admiration.[1] What finer subject for that hideous kind of art, which the cruelty of the times had brought into fashion, the representation of celebrated statues by *tableaux vivants?* An inscription and a fresco at Pompeii seem to prove that, when the criminal was a woman,[2] this terrible scene was often represented in the arena. Naked and bound by the hair[3] to the horns of a furious bull,[4] the miserable creatures glutted

---

287, 292. Helbig, *Wandgemälde*, Nos. 1151, 1152, 1153. Jahn, *Archæol. Zeitung*, 1853, Nos. 36 et seq.

[1] Pliny, xxxvi. v. (4). Vid. Brunn, quoted above, p. 129, note 3.

[2] "Videt... *memorandi spectaculi scenam* non tauro sed asino dependentem Dircen aniculam." Apul. *Metam.* vi. 127 (ed. Oudendorp, 435, 436). Conf. Lucian, *Lucius*, 23 (read γραῦν Δίρκην οὐκ ἐκ ταύρου ἀλλ' ἐξ ὄνου). Especially vid. *Memorie della R. Accademia Ercolanese*, vii. plate in the first Memoir, where the punishment seems to be represented as a spectacle (observation of M. Minervini).

[3] "Dircen ad taurum crinibus religatam necant." Hygin. *Fabulæ*, Feb. 8.

[4] Compare the punishment of St. Blandina, exposed in a net to a bull; and that of St. Perpetua and St. Felicita, also exposed

the lustful gaze of a savage people. Some of the Christian women thus immolated were feeble in body:[1] their courage was superhuman: but the infamous crowd had eyes only for their mangled bowels, their torn bosoms.

Next to the day on which Jesus died on Golgotha, the day of the festival in the gardens of Nero—we may fix it as the first of August, 64—was the most solemn in the history of Christianity. The solidity of a construction is in proportion to the sum of virtue, of sacrifice, of self-devotion, which has been built into its foundations. Only fanatics can found anything: Judaism still exists because of the intense ardour of its prophets and its zealots; Christianity, because of the courage of its first witnesses. The orgy of Nero was the great baptism of blood which marked out Rome, as the city of martyrs, to play a special part in the history of Christianity, and to become its second holy place. It was the taking possession of the Vatican Hill by a triumphant army

---

in a net to a mad cow. Letter in Euseb. *H.E.* v. 1. Martyrs of Africa, § 20.

[1] Clem. Rom. *Ad Cor.* i. 6.

of a kind which the world had not yet known. The hateful madman who governed the world did not perceive that he was the founder of a new order of things, and had signed for all future time a charter, the results of which would be claimed for mankind after the lapse of 1800 years.

IV.

I have already said that we can without improbability connect the deaths of the apostles Peter and Paul with the event which I have just narrated. The one historical fact by which we can explain the martyrdom of Peter is that of which Tacitus speaks.[1] Solid reasons lead us to believe that Paul also suffered martyrdom at Rome.[2] It is, then,

---

[1] *Ann.* xv. 44. Read attentively Clem. Rom. *Ad Cor.* i. § 5, 6, in the edition of Hilgenfeld. The πολὺ πλῆθος ἐκλεκτῶν, the Danaids and the Dirces certainly suffered at Rome; now these martyrs are, as it were, mingled up and confounded with the apostles Peter and Paul (συνηθροίσθη).

[2] The words of Clement of Rome, μαρτυρήσας ἐπὶ τῶν ἡγουμένων οὕτως ἀπηλλάγη τοῦ κόσμου, do not necessarily imply a violent death (conf. Acts xxiii. 11), but the whole of the passage, especially ἕως θανάτο [υ ἤλθον], in part conjectural, does prbably imply it, and the parallel with the μαρτυρήσας of Peter also

natural to refer his death also to the episode of July—August, 64.[1] As to the manner in which

---

indicates it. Dionysius of Corinth, Caius, priest of Rome, and Tertullian (*l.c.* note 1), believe that Paul suffered martyrdom. In the same way, the author of the Epistle of Ignatius to the Ephesians, § 12 (passage wanting in the Syriac). Conf. Commod. *Carmen*, 821.

[1] The strongest evidence of this is found in Clem. Rom. *Ad Cor.* i. 5, 6. The author of this Epistle, which was certainly written at Rome a few years after the death of the apostles (5, *initio*), probably between the years 93 and 96, establishes a connection between the execution of Peter and that of Paul, that of the πολὺ πλῆθος ἐκλεκτῶν, that of the Danaids and the Dirces, by the expression τούτοις τοῖς ἀνδράσιν συνηθροίσθη—implying a whole batch of irregular arrests—and, above all, by the common cause to which all these deaths are attributed, namely, "jealousy." Now it is clear that the πολὺ πλῆθος ἐκλεκτῶν, the Danaids and the Dirces, suffered in the persecution of July—August, 64. Dionysius of Corinth, quoted by Eusebius (*H.E.* ii. 25), says that Peter and Paul died at Rome about the same time (κατὰ τὸν αὐτὸν καιρόν); it is true that the force of his testimony is weakened by the tale which he seems to tell of Peter's apostolate at Corinth, and of the journeys of Peter and Paul in company. We detect in him the presence of a systematic theory, having for its object the association of Peter and Paul in the apostolate of the Gentiles. Tertull. *Praescr.* 36; *Adv. Marc.* iv. 5; and Commod. *Carmen*, 821, also associate the two apostles in their death. Conf. Iren. *Adv. Haer.* iii. i. 1, iii. 3. Euseb. *H.E.* ii. 22, 25, iii. 1. *Chron.* 13th year of Nero: Lactant. *De Mortibus Persecut.* 2. *Inst. Div.* iv. 21. Jerome, *De Viris ill.* 5. Euthalius, in Zaccagni, *Coll.*

the two apostles suffered, we know certainly that Peter was crucified.[1] According to some ancient

---

monum. vet. Eccl. Gr. p. 532. Sulpic. Sever. *Hist. Sacra*, ii. 29. Bede, *De rat. temp.* 303 (ed. Giles). All the Roman tradition (Caius, in Euseb. *H.E.* ii. 25). *Liber Pontificalis*, ed. Bianchini, articles *Peter* and *Cornelius;* but note the contradictions. Acts of Peter and Paul attributed to St. Linus, *Bibl. Max. patr.* ii. Pt. i. p. 69 c. Acts published by Tischendorf, § 84. Other Acts of Peter, quoted by Bosio, *Roma Sott.* 74 et seq., place the martyrdom or the grave of Peter in the circus of Nero ("inter duas metas, sub Terebintho, prope Naumachiam, in Vaticano, juxta obeliscum Neronis in monte, juxta Palatium Neronianum (the circus) in territorio triumphali"), that is, precisely in the place which was the scene of the atrocities of August, 64. (Vid. Platner and Bunsen, ii. i. 39—41.) Lastly, the tradition of Peter's crucifixion head downwards answers to Tacit. *Ann.* xv. 44. The belief that Peter and Paul suffered on the same day established itself at Rome, though not without dissent. (Council of Rome under Gelasius, Labbe, *Concil.* iv. col. 1262; Jerome, *De Viris ill.* 5.) Prudentius, St. Augustine and others, make the two apostles die on the same day of the calendar, with a year between them. Euseb. (*Chron.* ad ann. Neronis 13) and Jerome (*l.c.*) assign the death of both apostles to the year 68, but as the result of argument, not following tradition. Vid. Tillemont, *Mem.* i. note 40, on St. Peter. Zonaras, xi. 13. Laud, *Anecd. Syr.* i. 116.

[1] John xxi. 18, 19 (conf. John xii. 32, 33, xiii. 36). Tertull. *Adv. Marc.* iv. 5. *Præscr.* 36. *Scorpiace*, 15. Euseb. *H.E.* ii. 25. Lactant. *De Mortibus Persecut.* 2. Orosius, vii. 7. Note that Tacitus, *Ann.* xv. 44, counts *crucibus affixi* among those who suffered. It is true that alterations proposed in the text of this

texts, his wife died with him, and he saw her led out to execution.¹ A story accepted ever since the third century declares that, too humble to claim equality with Jesus, he begged to be crucified with his head downwards.² As the characteristic of the butchery of 64 was the invention of odious novelties in torture, it is possible that Peter may really have been exhibited to the mob in this horrible posture. Seneca mentions cases in which tyrants have been known to turn the heads of crucified persons earthwards.³ At a later period, Christian piety would see a mystic refinement⁴ in what was only a whimsical caprice of the executioner. Possibly the phrase of the fourth Gospel may contain some allusion to

---

passage (Bernays, 165, note 2) would strike out of the catalogue those who were only crucified; but Sulpicius Severus (ii. 29), who almost copies Tacitus, and a Tacitus more correct than ours, in agreement with Hermas (i. vis. iii. 2), expressly enumerates *cruces* (σταυροὺς) among the punishments.

[1] Clem. Alex. *Strom.* vii. 11.

[2] *Acta Petri et Pauli*, c. 81 (conf. Pseudo-Linus, 69, 70). Euseb. *H. E.* iii. 1 (after Origen). Euseb. *Dem. Ev.* iii. 5. Jerome, *De Viris ill.* 1.

[3] *Consol. ad Marciam*, 20 (written under Claudius).

[4] Rufin. transl. of Euseb. *H. E. l.c.*

the peculiarity of Peter's punishment:[1] "Thou shalt stretch forth thy hands, and another shall gird thee, and carry thee whither thou wouldst not." Paul, as belonging to a higher rank in society (*honestior*), had his head cut off.[2] It is possible also that he suffered after a regular process of trial,[3] and was not involved in the summary condemnation of the victims of Nero's festival.

All this, I repeat, is both doubtful and of no great importance. But true or not, the legend became an article of faith. At the beginning of the third century were already to be seen, not far from Rome, two monuments to which the names of the apostles Peter and Paul were attached. One, that of St. Peter, was situated at the foot of the Vatican Hill; the other, that of St. Paul, on the way to

---

[1] The girding of the loins with a napkin was by no means a rule in crucifixion. The passage in the *Gospel of Nicodemus*, Pt. i. A, ch. x., refers to a very modern conception of the crucifixion of Jesus.

[2] Tertull. *Præscr.* 36. *Scorp.* 15. Euseb. *H.E.* ii. 25. Lactant. *De Mortibus Persecut.* 2. Orosius, vii. 7. Euthalius in Zaccagni, 427, 522, 531—537. Conf. Paul, *Sentent.* xxix. 1.

[3] Clem. Rom. *Ad Cor.* i. 5, μαρτυρήσας ἐπὶ τῶν ἡγουμένων.

Ostia. They were called, in oratorical phrase, the "trophies" of the apostles.[1] They were probably *cellæ* or *memoriæ* dedicated to the two Saints. Similar monuments existed and were publicly recognized before the time of Constantine;[2] but we are to suppose that these "trophies" were known only to the faithful. Possibly they were no other than that Terebinth of the Vatican with which for ages the memory of Peter was associated, that Pine of the Aquæ Salviæ which was, according to one tradition, the centre of all recollections of Paul.[3] At a later period, these "trophies" became the tombs of the apostles. About the middle of the third century,

---

[1] Caius, quoted by Euseb. *H. E.* ii. 25. All that relates to the construction of the *memoriæ* of St. Peter at the Vatican by Anencletus (*Liber Pontificalis*, art. *Anencletus*) is legendary. Vid. Lipsius, *Chronol. der Röm. Bischöfe*, p. 269 et seq., comparing with it the text of Bianchini.

[2] Euseb. *Vita Const.* ii. 40. Conf. De Rossi, *Roma Sott.* 209, 210. The publicity of the Christian cemeteries is a fact beyond doubt.

[3] *Acta Petri et Pauli*, 80 (text of the MSS. of Paris, Tischendorf, p. 35 note). Nevertheless, the Aquæ Salviæ are too far from the Basilica of St. Paul without the Walls, to permit of the identification of the two sites.

two bodies, which universal veneration holds to be those of the apostles,[1] actually make their appear-

---

[1] *Kalendarium liberianum*, 3 Kal. Jun. (*Abh. der Kön. Sächs. Ges.* phil-hist. Class. i. 632). Inscription of Damasus, Gruter, ii. 1163. *Liber Pontificalis* (text of Bianchini and Lipsius (arts. *Peter, Cornelius, Damasus*, and all the articles from Linus to Victor, except two. The *Liber Pontificalis* contradicts itself. Nothing is more obscure than the removals of bodies made by St. Cornelius. It is said that he did no more than bring back the bodies of the apostles to their first resting-place. Why should they ever have been removed from it? The reason alleged, so far as the body of Peter is concerned, taken from Lamprid. *Heliog.* 23, has very little force, and none at all is brought forward in the case of Paul. The proximity of the Jewish cemetery of the Vigna Randanini inclines me to believe that the two bodies which were presented as those of the apostles were taken from the catacombs of the Appian Way by St. Cornelius (A.D. 251—253), at a time when the great persecution of Decius had raised the care of martyrs' bodies into an ecclesiastical duty, and had excited the zeal of the good Lucina, who was probably content with inconclusive proofs, and possibly could not refrain from committing some trifling pious frauds. The traditions as to the remaining of the bodies of the apostles at the catacomb of St. Sebastian, at the place which was called par excellence *Catacumbas* (κατὰ tumbas) Marchi, *Monum. delle arti Cristiane primitive*, 199—220), are thus explained. Vid. *Liber Pontificalis*, arts. *Cornelius, Damasus, Adrian I., Nicholas I.* Bede, *De temp. rat.* 309 (ed Giles). *Acts of St. Sebastian* and others. Bosio, 247, 248, 251—256, 259, 260. *Acta SS. Jan.* ii. 258, 278. Gruter, 1172, No. 12. De Rossi, *Roma Sott.* i. 236 et seq., 240, 242. *Catal. Imp. Rom.*

ance, brought most likely from the catacombs of the Appian Way, where there was more than one Jewish cemetery.[1] In the fourth century, those bodies repose where the two "trophies" stood.[2] Above

---

in Roncalli. *Vetustiora Lat. Script. Chronica* (Padua, 1787), ii. 248. Some MSS. of the *Acta Petri et Pauli* seem to wish to reconcile opposing accounts. Tischendorf, *Acta Apost. Apoc.* 38, 39, note. Lipsius, *Die Quellen der Röm. Petrussage*, 99. Mabillon, *Liturgia Gallicana*, 159. Conf. Gregory the Great, *Epist.* iv. xxx. (Opera, ii. col. 710, ed. Benedict.). Acts of Mar Scherbil, in Cureton, *Ancient. Syr. Docum.* 61 et seq. (trans.).

[1] Two are known to exist, at a distance of 200 or 300 metres, one to the north, the other to the south of the place (*ad Catacumbas*), whence, according to the tradition, the bodies of Peter and Paul were taken. De Rossi, *Bull.* 1867, pp. 3, 16. This is a strong reason for believing that the spot called κατὰ τυμβάs, or *ad tumbas*, which at the beginning of the third century was believed to contain the graves of the apostles, formed part of a vast subterranean Jewish cemetery, situated in the bend which the Appian Way makes near St. Sebastian. The centre of all the Christian burials of the three first centuries was in this region. De Rossi, *Roma Sott.* Vol. ii. *passim.*

[2] Euseb. *H.E.* ii. 25. Note that the meaning of κοιμητήριον is *tomb*. Eusebius admits that by τρόπαια Caius means tombs. The Roman tradition was almost in agreement as to the fact that both Peter and Paul had been buried near the place where they were put to death. Bosio, *Roma Sott.* 74 et seq., 197 et seq. In the case of martyrs, the place of execution and the place of burial were often confounded. Vid. Hegesipp. in Euseb. *H.E.*

the trophies are then raised two basilicas; one of which has become the present Basilica of St. Peter, while the other, that of St. Paul without the Walls, has preserved its main features down to our own day.

Did the "trophies" which the Christians venerated in the second century really designate the places at which the two apostles suffered? It is not unlikely that Paul, in the latter part of his life, inhabited the suburb which extended outside the Porta Lavernalis, on the road to Ostia.[1] On the

---

ii. xxiii. 18. *Liber Pontif.* arts. *Peter, Cornelius. Acta Petri et Pauli,* § 84. It is nevertheless probable that the above-named tradition arose from the fact that, after the final translation of the two bodies and the building of the basilicas, men were under the temptation to believe and say that the relics had always been on the spot where they were offered to the piety of the faithful. Conf. Euthalius in Zaccagni, 522, 523.

[1] Conf. *Kalendarium Lib. l.c. Liber Pontif.* art. *Cornelius. Acta Petri et Pauli,* 80. The place pointed out in these passages is the site of the Basilica of St. Paul, which has doubtless succeeded the τρόπαιον of Caius. It is at a comparatively modern epoch that the belief arose that St. Paul had been beheaded almost two miles further off, *Ad Aquas Salvias* or *Ad guttam jugiter manantem,* now St. Paul *alle tre Fontane,* one of the most striking scenes of the Roman Campagna. Gregory the Great,

other hand, the ghost of Peter, if Christian legend may be trusted, always wanders round the foot of the Vatican Hill, the gardens and the circus of Nero, and especially round the obelisk.[1] The reason of this is, if we choose to think so, that the circus in question preserved the remembrance of the martyrs of 64, with whom, in the absence of more precise evidence, Christian tradition associated Peter. We prefer to believe that there is some solid ground for the tradition,[2] and that the former place of the obelisk, now marked by an inscription, in the Sacristy of St. Peter's, indicates, with tolerable accuracy, the spot where Peter, in his frightful agony on the cross, glutted the eyes of a populace greedy of sights of suffering. But this is, after all, a question of very secondary importance. If the Vatican Basilica does not really cover the sepulchre of the

---

Epist. xiv. xiv. (Opp. ii. col. 1273, ed. Benedict.). *Acta Petri et Pauli*, 80 (according to some MSS., Tischendorf, 35, note). Acta SS. Junii, v. 43.

[1] Bosio, *Roma Sott.* 74 et seq. Lipsius, *Röm. Petrussage*, 102 et seq.

[2] The claims of S. Pietro in Montorio in regard to this matter are unsupported by evidence.

apostle Peter, it not the less points out to our recollection one of the most sacred sites of Christendom. The spot which the bad taste of the seventeenth century has occupied by a theatrical arcade was a second Calvary, which, even if it were not the place of Peter's crucifixion, saw—it is impossible to doubt it—the martyrdoms of the Danaids and the Dirces. We shall show in our next Lecture how legend resolved all these doubts, and in what way the Church concluded a reconciliation between Peter and Paul, which possibly had been already sketched out by the hand of death. This was the price at which success was to be bought. Apparently incapable of alliance, the Judeo-Christianity of Peter and the Hellenism of Paul were yet equally necessary to the success of the future work. Judeo-Christianity represented the conservative spirit, without which nothing is solid; Hellenism, the movement and the progress, without which nothing has any real existence. Life is the result of a conflict between these opposite forces. Death comes equally by excess or absence of the breath of revolution.

LECTURE III.

ROME, THE CENTRE OF GROWING ECCLESIASTICAL AUTHORITY.

LECTURE III.

ROME, THE CENTRE OF GROWING ECCLESIASTICAL AUTHORITY.

I.

Almost all the nations designed to play the part of civilizers on the great scale—as, for instance, Judea, Greece, the Italy of the Renaissance—exercise their full influence on the world only after they have fallen victims to their own greatness. They must first die: then the world lives by them, assimilating what they have created at the cost of their own fever and suffering. Nations, indeed, have to choose between the slow, quiet, obscure destiny of one who lives for himself, and the stormy and troubled career of one who lives for humanity. The people in the midst of which social and religious questions strive for solution, is almost always politically weak. Every country which dreams of a kingdom of God, which lives for general ideas, which attempts a work of universal concern, sacrifices in the act its particular fate, weakens and destroys its possibility of playing a great earthly part. No one, with impunity, can burn with an inward fire. In order that Judea might make a religious conquest of the world, it was necessary that she should be blotted out from the roll of nations. A revolution of extraordinary violence broke out in Judea in the year 66. For four years, the strange race which seems to have been created that it might distrust alike those who bless and those who curse it, was in a state of convulsion, before which the historian must pause with the respect due to all that is mysterious.

The causes of this crisis were of old standing, and the crisis itself inevitable. The Mosaic Law, the work of lofty idealists, possessed by a powerful socialistic thought, but the least politic of men, was, like Islam, exclusive of a civil society, existing side by side with the religious. This Law, which appears to have taken the form in which we now read it in the eighth century B.C., would, even if the Assyrian conquest had never taken place, have broken into fragments the little kingdom of the descendants of David. From the time that the prophetic element took the upper hand, the kingdom of Judah, on unfriendly terms with all its neighbours, full of enduring hatred for Tyre, at enmity with Edom, Moab and Ammon, had no longer any possibility of life in it. I repeat, a nation which devotes itself to social and religious problems, loses itself in politics. The day when Israel became "a peculiar treasure" unto God, "a kingdom of priests, a holy nation,"[1] it was decreed that it should never be a people like any other. It is impossible to unite contradictory destinies: excellence is always atoned for by abasement.

The empire of the Achæmenidæ gave Israel a brief repose. In this great feudal system, tolerant of all provincial differences, and strongly analogous to the Khalifat of Bagdad and the Ottoman Empire, the

---

[1] Exod. xix. 5, 6.

Jews found themselves more at ease than anywhere else. The rule of the Ptolemies, in the third century B.C., seems also to have been favourable to them. It was not so with the Seleucidæ. Under them, Antioch became the centre of an active Hellenic propaganda: Antiochus Epiphanes thought it his duty to mark his power by setting up everywhere the statue of the Olympian Zeus. Then broke out the first great Jewish rebellion against profane civilization. Israel had patiently borne the annihilation of his political existence from the time of Nabuchodonosor; but he was excited beyond all bounds when he saw his religious institutions in danger. A race, not generally warlike, was fired with heroic ardour: without regular army, without generals, without strategy, it overcame the Seleucidæ, maintained its revealed Law, and won for itself a second period of independence. At the same time, the Asmonean dynasty was always troubled by deep, inward vices: it lasted only for a century. The fate of the Jewish people was not to form a separate nationality: it is a race which always cherishes a dream of something that transcends nations: its ideal is not the city, but the synagogue, the free congregation. It is the same with Islam, which, while creating an immense empire, has at the same time destroyed all nationality—in the sense in which we understand the word—among its subjugated peoples, and has left them no other country than the mosque and the *zaouia*.

To such a social state the name of theocracy is often given, and rightly, if by that is understood that the basal idea of Semitic religion, and of the empires that have sprung from it, is the kingdom of God, regarded as the universal Sovereign and sole Master of the world. But among these peoples the word theocracy is not synonymous with the rule of priests. The priest, properly so called, plays only an unimportant part in the history of Judaism and of Islamism. Power belongs to the representative of God, to him whom God inspires, to the prophet, to the saint, to whoever has received a mission from heaven, and who proves his mission by the truest of all miracles, success. In default of a prophet, it attaches to the maker of apocalypses, and apocryphal books attributed to old prophets, to the doctor who interprets the Divine law, to the chief of the synagogue, more often still to the head of the family, who keeps the deposit of the Law, and hands it on to his children. Royalty, the civil power, do not count for much in a social organization of this kind. And such an organization never works better than when the individuals who submit themselves to it are spread abroad as tolerated strangers through a great and diverse empire. It is in the nature of Judaism, inasmuch as it cannot evolve from itself the principle of military power, to remain in a condition of political subordination. Its essence has been to form communities, which, with their code and their private magistracy, exist in the heart of other states, until modern liberalism introduces the principle of equality before the law.

The Roman rule, established in Judea in the year 63 B.C., by the arms of Pompey, seemed at first to realize some of the conditions of Jewish life. It was not at this period the policy of Rome to assimilate to herself the peoples which she annexed, one after the other, to her vast empire. While she took from them the right of peace and war, she claimed for herself only a deciding voice in great political questions. Under the last degenerate rulers of the Asmonean dynasty, as well as under the Herods, the Jewish nation preserved a semi-independence, in which its religious life was respected. But the moral crisis through which the people was passing was too violent. When men have reached a certain degree of religious fanaticism, they are ungovernable. It must also be admitted that the tendency of Rome always was to strengthen her rule in the East. The little vassal royalties, which she had at first preserved, disappeared from day to day, and the provinces were absorbed in the Empire. From the year 6 A.D., Judea was administered by procurators, who were subordinated to the imperial *legati* of Syria, and who governed side by side with the Herods. The impossibility of such a system made itself more manifest every day. The Herods, in the East, had no great reputation as men of genuine patriotism and piety. The administrative habits of the Romans, even on their most reasonable side, were hateful to the Jews. Generally speaking, the Romans showed the greatest consideration for the fastidious scruples of the nation; but this was not enough: things had come to such a pass that it was impossible to move in any direction without raising a question of Mosaic Law. Absolute religions, such as Islamism, Judaism, suffer no partition of authority. If they are not supreme, they complain that they are persecuted. If conscious of being protected, they grow exacting, and attempt to make life impossible to all religions round about them.

I should be leaving the path which I have marked out for myself if I were to tell you the story, as Josephus has preserved it, of that strange struggle, the terror in Jerusalem, with Simon Bar Gioras commanding the town, and John of Giskhala, and his assassins, master of the temple. Fanatical movements are far from excluding hatred, jealousy, mistrust, from the minds of those who are the actors in them: men of very deep and passionate convictions, when associated together, are prone to suspect each other. And this very fact constitutes a force; for mutual suspicion breeds terror among men, binds them together as with an iron chain, prevents moments of weakness and fallings away. It is only an artificial policy, one not based on conviction, which preserves the show of agreement and courtesy. Interest creates a coterie; principles make divisions, inspire the desire to expel, to decimate, to slay opponents. Those who bring superficial ideas to the judgment of human affairs, think that the revolution is lost when revolutionaries, as the phrase goes, begin to eat one another up. On the contrary, it is a proof that the revolution still possesses all its energy, and is directed by an impersonal ardour. Never was this more clearly seen than in the terrible drama of Jerusalem. The actors in it seem to have made a compact of mutual slaughter. As in those hellish revels in which, as the Middle Ages believed, Satan forms the ring, and drags towards a mysterious abyss long lines of men, dancing hand in hand to their fate, the revolution allows no one to fall out of the mad whirl which it leads. Behind the dancers is terror: by turns maddening and maddened, they approach the gulf: none can draw back, for behind each is a hidden sword, which, at the

very moment when he would willingly stop, drives him onward.

But what is strangest is, that these madmen are not altogether mistaken. The enthusiasts of Jerusalem, who at the very moment that she was in flames declared her to be eternal, were nearer the truth than the men who believed them to be only vulgar assassins. They were wrong as to the immediate military question, but right as to the far-off religious result. Those days of trouble really marked the moment at which Jerusalem became the spiritual capital of the world. The Apocalypse, the burning expression of the love which she inspired, has taken its place among the religious books of humanity, and has consecrated for ever the image of "the beloved city." Ah! we ought never to say beforehand who, in the time to come, is to be saint or scoundrel, fool or sage! Jerusalem, a city of ordinary citizens, would have developed, one cannot tell for how long, only an ordinary history. It was because she had the incomparable honour of being the cradle of Christianity that she was the victim of John of Giskhala and Simon Bar Gioras, in semblance the scourges of their country, in reality the instruments of her apotheosis. These zealots, whom Josephus regards as robbers and murderers, were politicians of the lowest class, incapable soldiers; but they heroically lost a country which it was impossible to save. They lost a material city; they opened the reign of the spiritual Jerusalem, more glorious in her desolation than in the days of Herod and of Solomon. What, indeed, did the conservatives, the Sadducees, desire? A paltry thing: the perpetuation of a city of priests, such as Emesa, Tyana, Comana. Of a truth, they were not wrong when they declared that the uprising of enthusiasm was the ruin of the nation. Revolution and Messianism destroyed the national existence of the Jewish people; but Revolution and Messianism were not the less that people's calling, the contribution which it made to the universal work of civilization.

II.

The victory of Rome was complete. A captain of our race, of our blood, a man like ourselves,[1] at

---

[1] The Flavii had their origin in Cisalpine Gaul. The portraits of Titus and Vespasian show us two ordinary faces, of the kind which we are most accustomed to see.

the head of legions, in whose muster-roll, if we could read it, we should find the names of more than one of our ancestors, had just crushed the fortress of Semitism, and inflicted on the theocracy, that formidable enemy of civilization, the greatest defeat which it had ever suffered. It was the triumph of the Roman Law, or rather of rational law—a product of philosophy which presupposed no revelation, over the Jewish *Thora*, the fruit of a revelation. This Law, of which the roots were partly Greek, but to the development of which the practical Latin genius had so largely contributed, was the admirable gift which Rome, in exchange for their independence, made to the nations whom she conquered. Every victory of Rome was a victory of reason. She offered to the world a principle, preferable in many respects to that of the Jews—I mean the principle of the secular state, resting upon a purely civil conception of society.

The triumph of Titus was, then, legitimate in more ways than one; and yet never was triumph less useful. The deplorable religious nullity of Rome rendered his victory unfruitful. It did not retard by a day the progress of Judaism: it did not give the religion of the Empire one chance the more of successful struggle against this formidable rival. The national existence of the Jewish people was irretrievably lost; but this was a piece of good fortune. The true glory of Judaism was the Christianity then in act of birth. And for Christianity, the destruction of Jerusalem and the temple was an advantage above all other.

If the reasoning which Tacitus ascribes to Titus is correctly reported,[1] the victorious general imagined that the destruction of the temple would be the ruin of Christianity as well as of Judaism. There never was a greater mistake. The Romans

---

[1] M. Jacob Bernays (*Ueber die Chronik des Sulpicius Severus*, Berlin, 1861, pp. 48 et seq.) has proved that the passage of Sulp. Sev. ii. xxx. 6, 7, is taken almost word for word from the lost portion of the *Histories* of Tacitus. Tacitus had himself derived his information from the book which Antonius Julianus, one of the officers of the Council of War, wrote under the title *De Judœis* (Minutius Felix, *Octav.* 33. Tillemont, *Hist. des Emp.* i. 588). Orosius, like Sulpicius Severus, had in his hands the complete text of the *Histories;* but he speaks vaguely, *diu deliberavit.* He ends, however, by attributing the fire to Titus, *incendit ac diruit* (vii. 9).

thought that in tearing away the root, they were at the same time tearing away the sucker; but the sucker had already become a tree, with an independent life of its own. If the temple had remained, Christianity would certainly have been arrested in its development. The temple, still standing, would have continued to be the centre of all Jewish activities. They would never have ceased to look upon it as earth's most sacred spot; to resort to it in pilgrimage; to bring thither their tribute. The church of Jerusalem, assembled about the sacred enclosure, would have continued, in virtue of its primacy, to receive the homage of the whole world, to persecute the Christians of the Pauline churches, to exact circumcision and the practice of the Mosaic Law from all who desired to call themselves disciples of Jesus. All fruitful missionary effort would have been forbidden: letters of obedience, signed at Jerusalem, would have been exacted from all wandering preachers.[1] A centre of infallible authority, a patriarchate, residing in a kind of College of Car

---

[1] See the letters at the head of the Pseudo-Clementine Homilies.

dinals, under the presidency of such persons as James, pure Jews, men belonging to the family of Jesus, would have been established,[1] and would have become an immense danger to the nascent Church. The very fact that Paul, after so much ill usage, always remains in connection with the church of Jerusalem, shows what difficulties would have attended a rupture with those holy personages. Such a schism would have been thought an enormity. Separation from Judaism would have been impossible, and yet that separation was the necessary condition of the existence of the new religion, as the cutting of the umbilical cord is the condition of the

---

[1] In our own time, an analogous state of things is producing itself in connection with Judaism, and seems likely to acquire considerable importance. The Jews of Jerusalem all pass for *hakamim*, or learned men, having no other occupation than meditation upon the Law. As such, they have a right to alms, and look upon themselves as entitled to support from Jews of the whole world. Beggars on their behalf go about all the East, and even the rich Israelites of Europe conceive themselves obliged to assist their needs. On the other side, the decisions of the Great Rabbi of Jerusalem tend to acquire universal authority, although formerly all doctors were equal, or at all events their credit depended on their reputation. In this way it is possible that at some future time Jerusalem may become the doctrinal centre of Judaism.

existence of a new being. The mother would have killed the child. On the other hand, the temple once destroyed, the Christians no longer bear it in mind: before long they will look upon it as a profane spot:[1] Jesus will be all in all to them.

By the same blow, the Christian church at Jerusalem was reduced to a secondary importance. It is seen to form itself anew around the centre from which its strength proceeds, the *desposyni*, the members of the family of Jesus, the sons of Cleopas; but its day of royalty is past. This focus of hatred and exclusiveness once destroyed, the mutual approach of opposing parties in the church of Jesus will become easy. Peter and Paul will be reconciled of their own accord, and the terrible duality of nascent Christianity will cease to be a mortal wound. Lost in the depths of Batanea, of the Hauran, the little group which attached itself to the kinsmen of Jesus, to James, to Cleopas, becomes the Ebionite sect and slowly disappears.

---

[1] "Ecclesia Dei jam per totum orbem uberrime germinante, hoc (templum) tanquam effœtum ac vacuum nullique usui bono commodum arbitrio Dei auferendum fuit." Orosius, vii. 9.

These kinsmen of Jesus were pious people, quiet, mild, modest, labouring with their hands,[1] faithful to the severest principles of Jesus in regard to poverty,[2] but at the same time very rigid Jews, who prized above every other advantage the title of children of Israel.[3] Men held them in great reverence, giving them a name the Greek equivalent of which was δεσπόσυνοι. From the year 70 to about the year 110, they virtually governed the churches beyond Jordan, and formed a kind of Christian senate. The immense danger to nascent Christianity involved in these genealogical prejudices needs no proof. A species of Christian noblesse was in course of formation. In the political order, a nobility is almost necessary to the state, for politics have to do with coarse contentions which make them more a material than an ideal thing. A state is thoroughly strong only when a certain number of communities,

---

[1] Hegesippus in Euseb. *H. E.* iii. 20.

[2] Gospel of the Hebrews, ed. Hilgenfeld, 16, 17, 25. *Recognit.* ii. 29.

[3] Of this St. James furnished the ideal. See the Epistle attributed to him.

in the exercise of a traditional privilege, acknowledge it to be both their interest and their duty to attend to its affairs, to represent it, to defend it. But in the ideal order, birth is nothing: the measure of each man's value is furnished by the truth which he discovers and the good which he realizes. Institutions which have a religious, literary, moral object, are ruined when considerations of family, caste, heredity, come to prevail in them. The nephews and the cousins of Jesus would have caused the destruction of Christianity, if the Pauline churches had not already been strong enough to act as a counterpoise to this aristocracy, the tendency of which would have been to confine respectability to itself, and to have treated all converts as intruders. Claims such as those which the descendants of Ali put forward in Islam would have been made. Islam would certainly have perished in the troubles caused by the family of the Prophet, if the result of the struggles of the first century of the Hegira had not been to push back into the second rank all who had held a place too near the person of the founder. The true heirs of a great man are not his kinsmen in blood, but those who continue his work. Looking on the tradition of Jesus as their own private property, the little coterie of Nazarenes would have certainly smothered it. Happily, this narrow circle disappeared before long: in the depths of the Hauran, the kinsmen of Jesus were soon forgotten. They lost all importance, and Jesus was left to his true family, to the only family whom he ever acknowledged, those who "hear the word of God and keep it."[1] Many passages in the Gospels, in which the family of Jesus is represented in a light that can hardly be called favourable, possibly arose from the antipathy which the aristocratic pretensions of the *desposyni* could not fail to inspire in those around them.

III.

In proportion as the Church of Jerusalem falls, the Church of Rome rises; or to put the fact in a better way, a phenomenon that plainly shows itself in the years that follow the victory of Titus is, that the Church of Rome becomes more and more the

---

[1] Luke xi. 28.

heir of the Church of Jerusalem, and takes its place. The spirit of the two Churches is the same; but what was a danger at Jerusalem becomes an advantage at Rome. The taste for tradition and hierarchy, the respect for authority, are in some sort transplanted from the courts of the Temple to the West. James, the brother of the Lord, had been a quasi Pope at Jerusalem; Rome is about to take up the part of James. We are to have the Pope of Rome; without Titus we should have had the Pope of Jerusalem. But there is this great difference between them, that while the Pope of Jerusalem would have smothered Christianity at the end of a century or two, the Pope of Rome has made it the religion of the world.

The truth of what I have said is illustrated in a very important personage, who appears to have been at the head of the Roman Church in the last years of the first century, and in regard to whom I am happy to find myself in accord with one of your ablest and most enlightened critics, Dr. Lightfoot:[1]

---

[1] *St. Clement of Rome: with an Appendix containing the newly-recovered portions;* with Introductions, Notes and Transla-

I mean Clement of Rome. In the half shadow in which he remains, enveloped and as it were lost in the luminous dust of a fine historic distance, Clement is one of the great figures of a nascent Christianity: we might liken him to some head in fresco of Giotto's, old and faded, but still to be recognized by its golden glory and the pure and mild brilliance of its indistinct features.

Everything leads us to believe that Clement was of Jewish origin.[1] He seems to have been born at Rome, of one of those Palestinian families which for one or more generations had inhabited the capital of the world.[2] His knowledge of cosmography[3]

---

tions: London, 1877. The system of the school of Tübingen in regard to Clement is deeply impressed with a character of subtlety and exaggeration.

[1] Note especially, in his letter, the expression, ὁ πατὴρ ἡμῶν Ἰακώβ (ch. 4), and what he says of the temple of Jerusalem (ch. 40, 41).

[2] Ch. 40, 41. The author of the latter speaks of the temple as standing, although he knew it only from books.

[3] See especially ch. 20, and in particular the passage upon "the worlds lying behind the ocean." Note the comparison of the Phœnix, ch. 29.

and secular history[1] testifies to a careful education. Without having any decisive proof of the fact, we may admit that he had been at an early period in relation with the apostles, and especially with Peter.[2] The high rank which he held in the purely spiritual hierarchy of the Church of his times, and the unequalled credit which he enjoyed, are beyond doubt. His approval was a law in itself.[3] All parties claimed his leadership and desired to shelter themselves beneath his authority. It is probable that he was one of the chief actors in the great work which was in process of accomplishment—I mean the posthumous reconciliation of Peter and Paul, and the fusion of the two parties,—a fusion without which the work of Christ must have perished. He is the first type of Pope which Church history presents to us. His lofty personality, which

---

[1] Ch. 55.

[2] Irenæus, *l. c.* Irenæus requires the reality of these relations to support his thesis as to the apostolical tradition. Tertull. *Præscr.* 32. Origen, *De Princ.* ii. 6. Rufinus, *De adult. libr. Orig.* p. 50 (Delarue, Vol. iv. app.).

[3] Pseudo-Hermas, vis. ii. 4.

legend makes more lofty still, was, after that of Peter, the holiest figure of primitive Christian Rome. Succeeding ages looked upon his venerable face as that of a mild and grave legislator, a perpetual homily of submission and respect.

Already the idea of a certain primacy belonging to his Church was beginning to make its way to the light. The right of warning other churches and of composing their differences was conceded to it. Similar privileges—so at least it was believed[1]—had been accorded to Peter by the other disciples. Thus a bond which gradually grew closer was established between Peter and Rome. Grave dissensions tore in pieces the Church of Corinth.[2] The Roman Church, consulted as to these troubles, replied in a letter which is still extant. It is anonymous, but a very ancient tradition assigns the composition of it to Clement.

The Church of Corinth had changed very little since the time of Paul. Its spirit of pride, of disputation, of fickleness, was the same. We feel that the principal opposition to the hierarchy arose from

---

[2] Luke xxii. 32.
[3] Hegesipp. in Euseb. *H.E.* iii. 16, iv. 22.

the Greek character, always mobile, undisciplined, unable to convert a mob into a flock. Women, children were in full revolt. Transcendental doctors fancied themselves in possession of profound views upon every subject, of mystic secrets, analogous to the "speaking with tongues" and the "discernment of spirits." Those who were honoured by these supernatural gifts despised the *presbyteri*, and aspired to take their place. Corinth had a respectable body of presbyters, but one which did not aim at high mysticism. The claim of the illuminated was to cast it into the shade and to assume its office: some *presbyteri* were actually deprived.[1] The struggle began between the established hierarchy on one side and personal revelations on the other, a struggle which is to fill all the history of the Church; for the privileged soul always finds it hard to bear that, in spite of the favours with which it is honoured, a clergy which is at once coarse-minded and ignorant of the spiritual life should authoritatively rule it. Finally, the innovators, proud to excess of their lofty virtue,

---

[1] Clem. Rom. *Ad Cor.* i. c. 44.

exalted chastity to the point of depreciating marriage.¹ It was, as we see, the heresy of individual mysticism, maintaining the rights of the spirit against authority, and, on the strength of direct relations with the Deity, claiming superiority over common mortals and the ordinary clergy.

The Roman Church was henceforth the Church of order, of rule, of subordination. Its fundamental principle was, that humility and submission were of more account than the sublimest gifts.² Its letter to the Corinthians is the first manifesto of the principle of authority made within the Christian Church.³

---

[1] Clem. Rom. *Ad Cor.* i. ch. 38, 48. Conf. ch. 1, 21.

[2] Clem. Rom. *Ad Cor.* i. ch. 38, 48.

[3] Few writings are as authentic. Dionys. of Corinth (in Eus. *H.E.* iv. xxiii. 11). Hegesipp. (in Eus. *H.E.* iii. xvi. iv. xxii. 1). Iren. (*Adv. Hær.* iii. iii. 3). Clem. Alex. (*Strom.* i. 7, iv. 17—19, v. 12, vi. 8). Origen (*De Princ.* ii. 6. *Selecta in Ezech.* viii. 3. Opp. Vol. iii. 422. *In Johann.* i. 28. Opp. Vol. vi. 36, iv. 153). Euseb. (*H.E.* iii. xvi. xxxviii. 1, vi. xiii. 6). Down to a recent date, the work was known only by the celebrated *Codex Alexandrinus* in the British Museum. In this copy there were two pages wanting. In 1879, Philotheus Bryennius, Metropolitan of Serræ, published it in a complete form, after a MS. of the library of St. Sepulchre, in the Fanar (Constantinople, 8vo). Vid. the recent publications of Hilgenfeld, of Gebhardt and

Some years ago, a great outcry was raised against a French Archbishop, then a senator, who said from the tribune, "My clergy is my regiment." Clement had said the same thing long before. Order and obedience—this is the supreme law of the family and of the church. "Let us consider the soldiers who serve under our sovereigns,[1] with what order, what punctuality, what submission, they execute the com-

---

Harnack (Leipzig, 1876), of Lightfoot (London, 1877). In the Cod. Alex. the work is expressly attributed to Clement (index at the beginning of the volume). In the MS. of the Fanar, the same ascription forms part of the title-page. The pretended second letter to the Corinthians, preserved in the same volumes, and complete only in the second, is not by Clement. Irenæus (*l. c.*), Clem. Alex. (*Strom.* v. 12), Origen, speak of only one letter of Clement's to the Corinthians. Conf. Euseb. *H. E.* iii. 38. Jerome, *De Vir. ill.* 16. Photius, cxii. cxiii. The so-called second Epistle is rather a sermon than a letter. It belongs to the second century. Vid. *Journal des Savants*, Jan. 1877. Other unauthentic letters circulated under the sanction of the name of Clement. Epiph. *Hær.* xxii. 6, xxx. 15. Hilgenfeld, *N. T. extra Can. Rec.* i. 61, 74—76. Conf. *Zeitsch. für Kirchengeschichte*, i. 272 et seq., 329 et seq.

[1] Ch. 37. It has been proposed to read τοῖς ἡγουμένοις αὐτῶν. But the two MSS. have ἡμῶν. Besides, the passage in ch. 61, wanting in the Cod. Alex., in agreement with the Syriac, τοῖς τε ἄρχουσι καὶ ἡγουμένοις ἡμῶν, fully justifies the reading of ch. 37. Vid. *Journal des Savants*, Jan. 1877, pp. 8, 9.

mands given to them. All are not prefects, or tribunes, or centurions, but each in his own rank obeys the orders of the emperor and his leaders. The great cannot exist without the small, nor the small without the great. In all things there is a mixture of different elements, and in this mixture there is profit. Let us take our body as an example. The head without the feet is nothing, nor the feet without the head. The least of our organs are necessary and serve the whole body; all conspire together and obey one principle of subordination for the preservation of the whole."

The history of the ecclesiastical hierarchy is one of a three-fold abdication: first, the community of the faithful abandoning all power to the elders or *presbyteri;* the presbyteral body then concentrating itself in a single person, who is the *episcopos;* finally, the *episcopi* of the Latin Church recognizing one among themselves, the Pope, as chief. This last stage of progress, if progress it can be called, has been reached only in our own day. The creation of the episcopate is the work of the second century. The absorption of the Church by the *presbyteri* was an accomplished fact before the end of the first. In the Epistle of Clement of Rome, it is not the episcopate, but the presbyteral body, which is in question.[1] We find no trace as yet of a *presbyteros* superior to and about to dethrone the rest. But the author loudly proclaims that the presbyters, the clergy, are anterior to the people. The apostles, in founding churches, have chosen by the inspiration of the Holy Ghost "the bishops and deacons of the believers that are to be." The powers proceeding from the apostles have been transmitted by a regular succession. No church, therefore, has the right of depriving its elders.[2] In the church, the rich have no privileges. In like manner, those who have been favoured with mysterious gifts, far from thinking themselves above the hierarchy, ought to be most submissive.

Men were approaching the great question, "What is the essential element in the Church? Is it the

---

[1] Ch. 39. The words πρεσβύτεροι, ἐπίσκοποι (ch. 42, 44) are synonymous in our Epistle, as in Phil. i. 1; Acts xx. 17 et seq., 28. The words ἡγούμενοι, προηγούμενοι have the same meaning. Conf. Heb. xiii. 7, 17, 24.

[2] Ch. 44.

people? the clergy? the inspired soul?" The question had been already asked in Paul's time, and he had solved the problem in the only true way, namely, by mutual charity. Our Epistle solves it in the sense of pure Catholicism. The apostolical credential is everything: the right of the people is reduced to nothing. We may well say, therefore, that Catholicism had its origin in Rome, for it was the Roman Church that first formulated its law. Precedence does not belong to spiritual gifts, or to science, or to distinction; it belongs to the hierarchy, to powers transmitted by the channel of canonical ordination, attaching itself to the apostles by an unbroken chain. Men felt that the free Church, such as Jesus had conceived it,[1] such as Paul still understood it to be,[2] was an anarchic Utopia, holding no promise of the future. With evangelical liberty, disorder went hand in hand: they did not see that, in the long run, hierarchy meant uniformity and death.

---

[1] Matt. xviii. 20.   [2] 2 Cor. i. 21.

IV.

I look upon the Gospel of Luke as having been written at Rome at no great distance from the social circle of which Clement was a member. Clement had probably seen neither Peter nor Paul.[1] His large practical good sense showed him that, for the safety of the Christian Church, the reconciliation of the two founders was necessary. Did he inspire St. Luke, who appears to have stood in some kind of relation to him, or did these two pious souls spontaneously agree as to the direction which it was expedient to give to Christian opinion? We have no records which enable us to answer the question. All that we certainly know is, that the reconciliation was the work of Rome.[2] Rome had two churches, one descending from Peter, the other from Paul. To the numerous converts who came to Jesus, these by the channel of the school of Peter, those by the

---

[1] Legend makes him sometimes the disciple of Peter, sometimes of Paul.

[2] Note in Luke the Latin words, τρίστεγος, σουδάρια, σιμικίνθια.

channel of the school of Paul, and who were equally tempted to cry, "What, are there then two Christs?" it was necessary to be able to say, "No; Peter and Paul were absolutely at one: the Christianity of the one is the Christianity of the other." It may be that with this view a turn was given to the evangelical legend of the miraculous draught of fishes.[1] According to the account of Luke, the nets of Peter were not large enough to hold the multitude of fishes that were willing to be taken: Peter is obliged to call his fellow-fishermen to his aid: a second boat, that of Paul and his friends, is filled like the first, and the take of the kingdom of God is large to overflowing.

The lives of the two apostles began to fade away from men's minds. All who had known them were gone, and for the most part without leaving any record behind. Upon this virgin canvas men were free to paint what picture they would. Friends and enemies alike took advantage of the general ignorance to invent arguments in support of their theories

---

[1] Luke v. 1—11. Conf. Mark i. 14, 19; Matt. iv. 12—17.

and to gratify their animosities. A vast Ebionite legend arose in Rome, and, under the name of "The Preaching" or "The Journeys of Peter," took a fixed shape about the year 130 A.D., that is to say, 66 years, more or less, after the death of the apostles.[1] The journeys and the preaching of Peter were its main subject. It told of the mission of the head of the apostles, chiefly on the coast of Phœnicia, the conversions which he had effected, and his struggles, especially with the great Antichrist, Simon of Gitton, who at this time was the spectre of the Christian consciousness. But often, in ambiguous phrase, another person was indicated under this abhorred name—the false apostle Paul, the enemy of the Law, the destroyer of the true Church.[2] And the true Church was that of Jerusalem, with James, the brother of the Lord, at its head. No

---

[1] Vid. Lipsius, *Römische Petrussage*, already quoted.

[2] Vid. *Homilies*, ii. 17, 22 et seq., xvi. 15, 16, xvii. 17, 18, 19 (conf. Gal. ii. 11). It is beyond doubt, whatever the critics of the Tübingen school may say, that Simon of Gitton was a real person, and that he often figures on his own account in the Pseudo-Clementine romance, as we have it. But the passages above quoted cannot refer exclusively to him.

apostleship was worth anything unless it could show letters proceeding from this central college. Paul had no such letters: he was therefore an intruder into the fold. He was the "enemy" who followed the steps of the true sower that he might sow tares.[1] With what force, then, did Peter lay bare his impostures, his lying stories of personal revelations, his ascent into the third heaven,[2] his pretence of knowing about Jesus what the hearers of the gospel had not heard, the exaggerated conception which he and his disciples cherished of the divinity of Jesus![3] At Antioch, above all, the triumph of Peter was complete. Simon had succeeded in turning away the people of that city from the truth. By a series of clever manœuvres, Peter induces a victim of Simon's enchantments, to whom the magician had given his own likeness, to recant in these words:

---

[1] Matt. xiii. 24 et seq. Epiph. *Hær.* xxx. 16, seems to imply Ebionite writings in which Paul was referred to by name.

[2] *Recogn.* ii. 65. Conf. 2 Cor. xi. 14 with *Recogn.* ii. 18; the σκεῦος ἐκλογῆς of *Recogn.* iii. 49 with Acts ix. 15, &c. Note also *Acta Petri et Pauli*, ch. 63—66.

[3] *Homilies*, xvi. xvii. xviii.

"I have lied as to Peter: he is the true apostle of the Prophet sent by God for the salvation of the world. This night angels have scourged me for my calumnies against him. Do not listen to me if, after this, I speak against him."[1] Naturally, all Antioch returns to Peter, and curses his rival.

These eccentricities of ignorant sectaries would have passed away without result anywhere but at Rome; but in the capital of the world whatever related to Peter was of importance. In spite of its heresies, the book of "The Preaching of Peter" was deeply interesting to the orthodox. In it was proclaimed the primacy of Peter. It was insulting, it is true, to St. Paul, but a touch here and there might tone down whatever was offensive in its attack. Many attempts, therefore, were made to lessen the singularities of the new book, and to adapt it to Catholic wants. This fashion of remoulding books, to adapt them to the opinions of a sect, was common and approved.[2] Little by little, the force of circumstances made itself felt: all sensible men saw that

---

[1] *Homilies*, xx. 12—23. [2] *Contestatio Jac.* 5.

the only salvation for the work of Jesus lay in completely reconciling the two chiefs of Christian preaching. Even so late as the fifth century, Paul still had implacable enemies in the Nazarenes; and in the same way he had fanatical disciples like Marcion. But between these obstinate sections, on the right hand and on the left, there was a fusion of many moderate men who, though owing their Christianity to one of the two schools and remaining attached to it, fully recognized the right of others to call themselves Christians. James, the partizan of an uncompromising Judaism, was sacrificed; although he would have been the true chief of the circumcision, Peter, who had shown himself much less offensive to the disciples of Paul, was preferred before him. It is only among the Jewish Christians that James still retained a few fiery partizans.[1]

It is difficult to say who gained most by this reconciliation. The concessions came principally from the side of Paul: all his disciples admitted the claims of Peter without difficulty, while the majority

---

[1] Epiph. *Hær.* xxx. 16.

of Christians repudiated Paul. But concessions are usually made by the strong. In reality, each day as it came gave the victory to Paul. Every Gentile that was converted weighed down the balance on his side. Except in Syria, the Jewish Christians were, as it were, drowned in the flood of new converts. The Pauline churches prospered: they had a good sense, a solidity of mind, pecuniary resources, which the others had not. The Ebionite churches, on the contrary, grew poorer from day to day. The money of the Pauline churches was applied to keep alive the boastful poor, who, though unable to earn their own livelihood, possessed the living tradition of the primitive spirit. Whatever there was among them of lofty piety, of severe morals, the Christian communities of heathen origin admired, imitated, made their own. Before long it came to this, that so far as the most eminent personages of the Church of Rome were concerned, no distinction could be made. The mild and conciliatory spirit which had once been represented by Clement of Rome and St. Luke, prevailed. The treaty of peace was sealed. It was agreed, in conformity with the system of the author of the Acts,[1] that Peter had converted the first fruits of the Gentiles, and had taken the lead in freeing them from the yoke of the Law.[2] It was admitted that Peter and Paul had been the two chiefs, the two founders of the Church of Rome. They became the two members of an inseparable pair, twin luminaries like the sun and moon. What one taught, the other had taught also: they had always been at one: they had combated the same enemies: they had both been victims of the treachery of Simon the Magician: at Rome they had lived like two brothers: the Church of Rome had been their common work.[3] The supremacy of that Church was in this way established for ages to come.[4]

From the reconciliation of parties and the lulling to rest of primitive dissensions, there resulted a grand unity—the Catholic Church, the Church at once of Peter and of Paul, ignorant of the rivalries which had marked the first century of Christianity. The churches of Paul had manifested most of the spirit

---

[1] Acts x. xv. 7.   [2] Acts xv. 7 et seq.
[3] *Acta Petri et Pauli*, 5, 22, 26, 60, 72.   Conf. 2 Peter ii. 9.
[4] Irenæus, *Adv. Hær.* iii. iii. 2.

of conciliation, and it was they who triumphed. The obstinate Ebionites remained in Judaism, and shared its immobility. Rome was the point at which this great transformation was effected. Already the high Christian destiny of this wonderful city was writing itself in luminous characters.

The deaths of the two apostles, in especial, occupied the minds of both parties, and gave occasion to very various manipulations of the story. The web of legend was woven by an instinctive force, almost as little to be resisted as that which had directed the formation of the legend of Jesus. The end of the life of Peter and Paul was determined *à priori*. It was maintained that Christ had announced the martyrdom of Peter, as he had predicted the death of the sons of Zebedee.[1] Men felt a desire to associate in death the two men whose reconciliation they had compelled. It was wished—and here, perhaps, the wish was not far from the truth—that they should die together, or at all events in connection with the same train of circumstances. The places

---

[1] John xii. 32, 33, xiii. 36, xxi. 18, 19. Conf. Matt. xx. 22, 23; Mark x. 38, 39.

which were believed to have been sanctified by this bloody drama were early fixed upon, and consecrated by *memoriæ*. In cases of this kind, what the people wishes always prevails in the end. Legend retrospectively makes history what it ought to have been, but what it never really is. Only recently, there was no place of popular resort in Italy where the portraits of Victor Emmanuel and Pius IX. were not to be seen side by side; and the general belief would have it that these two men—the representative of the principles whose reconciliation an almost universal feeling thinks necessary to Italy—were at the bottom on very good terms. If in our age such views were allowed to impress themselves upon history, we should read some day, in documents making a serious claim upon our belief, that Victor Emmanuel, Pius IX.—and Garibaldi would probably make the third—saw one another secretly, understood one another, loved one another. The association of Voltaire with Rousseau has been brought about by necessities of the same kind. In like manner, in the middle ages, it was repeatedly sought to prove, with a view of appeasing the hatred of the Dominicans and the Franciscans, that the founders of these two orders had been like two brothers, living together in the most affectionate relations, that their two rules had been at first but one, and that St. Dominic had girded himself with the cord of St. Francis.[1]

In all that concerns Peter and Paul, the work of legend was rich and rapid. Rome, with all its suburbs—and especially the road to Ostia—was full of recollections which claimed to have their origin in the last days of the two apostles. A host of touching circumstances—the flight of Peter, the vision of Jesus bearing his cross, the *iterum crucifigi*, the last farewell of Peter and Paul, Peter's meeting with his wife, Paul at the Aquæ Salviæ, Plautilla sending the kerchief with which her hair was tied to bind the eyes of Paul—all this made a beautiful narrative, which only wanted a narrator, a man at once of genius and a simple mind. But it was too late: the vein of the first Christian literature was

---

[1] Dante, *Parad.* xi. 28 et seq. Wadding, *Ann.* i. 293 et seq., iii. 380 et seq. *Acta SS. Maii*, ii. 827 et seq. *Aug.* i. 442, 484 et seq., 960, 976. *Oct.* ii. 869 et seq., 876 et seq.

exhausted: the serenity of the author of the Acts was lost: it was impossible to rise to a higher tone than that of legend and romance. It was impossible to choose among a host of versions equally apocryphal: it was useless to seek to place these feeble narratives under the shelter of the most venerable names (Pseudo-Linus, Pseudo-Marcellus): the Roman legend of Peter and Paul never emerged from the sporadic stage. It was recounted by pious guides rather than seriously read. It was a purely local matter: no version of it was set apart to be read in churches: none became authoritative.

Almost all of you will some day go to Rome, or, if you have already been there, will return once more. Well, if you retain any recollection of these Lectures, go, in memory of me, to the Aquæ Salviæ, *alle Tre Fontane*, beyond St. Paul without the Walls. It is one of the most beautiful spots in the Roman Campagna, solitary, moist, green and sad. A deep depression in the soil, crowned by those grand horizontal lines which no sign of life disturbs, thither brings a spring of clear and cold water. Fever is in the air we breathe, the humidity of the grave. There the monks of La Trappe have established themselves, and conscientiously pursue their religious suicide. Sit there awhile—not too long—and while the Trappist gives you to drink of the water which rises from the three fountains that mark where Paul's head struck the earth, think of him who came to talk of these legends with you, and to whom you listened so courteously and with so kind an attention.

LECTURE IV.

ROME, THE CAPITAL OF CATHOLICISM.

I.

LECTURE IV.

ROME, THE CAPITAL OF CATHOLICISM.

In the primitive Christian community, the importance of Churches was in proportion to their apostolical nobility: nothing could be simpler. The guarantee of orthodoxy was the *diadoche*, the episcopal succession by which the great Churches were connected with the apostles. A direct succession was a very strong warrant of agreement in doctrine; the greatest possible importance was attached to it. But what shall we say of a Church founded both by Peter and by Paul? It is clear that such a Church would be regarded as having a real superiority over all others. To have succeeded in establishing this belief was the masterpiece of that cleverness which characterized the Church of Rome. By the time of Antoninus Pius, almost everybody had come to believe that Peter and Paul had, in perfect agreement, founded Christianity at Rome, and had sealed the work with their blood. The ecclesiastical destiny of Rome was thenceforth fixed. When her part in the profane world was played out, this extraordinary city was destined to play another and a sacred part, a part like that of Jerusalem. The Christianity which she has so cruelly fought against, she will succeed in turning to her own advantage. So hardly does humanity escape from those upon whom fortune has laid the great secular task *regere imperio populos !*

Rome, under Antoninus Pius and Marcus Aurelius, was at the epoch of her highest greatness:[1] her world-wide rule seemed uncontested: no cloud was to be seen upon the horizon. Far from slackening, the movement which impelled provincials, especially from the East, to crowd within her walls, increased in intensity. The Greek-speaking population was

---

[1] De Rossi, *Piante iconografiche e prospettiche ai Roma* (Rome, 1879), pp. 46 et seq. The customs' limit of Marcus Aurelius determined the circuit of the wall of Aurelian—that is to say, of the actual enclosure.

more numerous than it had ever been. The insinuating *græculus*, with his universal cleverness, drove the Italian out of great households: Latin literature declined from day to day: Greek became the literary, religious, philosophical language of the enlightened, as it was already the dialect of the lower classes. The importance of the Church of Rome was measured by that of the city itself. Hyginus, its head, enjoyed the respect of all Christendom. Whoever wished to make a place for himself in the eye of the world aspired to come to Rome: nothing was consecrated that had not taken a certificate at this universal exhibition of the products of the universe.

Gnosticism, with its ambition to set the fashion of Christian preaching, especially yielded to this impulse. No Gnostic school had its origin in Rome, but almost all came thither to fail. Valentinus was the first who tried the adventure. It is even possible that this audacious sectary may have cherished the idea of seating himself on the episcopal throne of the unrivalled city. He showed himself with all the external appearances of Catholicism, and preached in the eccentric fashion of which he was the inventor.

His success was not great: his pretentious philosophy, his restless curiosity, scandalized the faithful. Hyginus drove the innovator from the Christian pulpit. From that time forward the Roman Church gave tokens of the purely practical tendency which was ever afterwards to distinguish her, and showed herself ready to sacrifice, without regret, knowledge and ability to edification.

The centre of a future Catholic orthodoxy was plainly here. Pius, who succeeded Hyginus, showed the same firmness in defending the purity of the faith. Cerdo, Marcion, Valentinus, Marcellinus, are removed from the Church by the sentence of Pius. In the reign of Antoninus, the germ of the Papacy already exists in a very definite form. The Church of Rome shows itself increasingly indifferent to those visionary speculations which were the delight of minds full of the intellectual activity of the Greeks, but at the same time corrupted by the dreams of the East. The organization of Christian society was the chief work pursued at Rome. That wonderful city brought to this task the exclusively practical genius and the powerful moral energy which she has applied in so many different ways. Almost careless of speculation, decisively hostile to novelties of doctrine, she presided as a mistress already practised in the art, over all the changes which took place in the discipline and the hierarchy of the Church.

I.

What was in process of development in the Christian Church, about the year 120 or 130, was the episcopate. Now the creation of the episcopate was evidently the work of Rome. Every *ecclesia* supposes a little hierarchy, a committee, as we say now, a president, assessors, and a small staff of servants. Democratic clubs take care that these offices shall be held for as short a time and confer as little power as possible; but the result of this is a character of precariousness attaching to their action, so that no club ever survives the circumstances which have called it into existence. The Jewish synagogue was a much more continuous thing, although its staff never developed into a clergy. This was partly the result of the subordinate position which for centuries Judaism occupied: pressure from without counteracted the effect of divisions within. Under the same absence of direction, the Christian Church would no doubt have failed to fulfil its destiny. If men had continued to look upon ecclesiastical powers as emanating from the Church itself,[1] the Church would have lost all its hieratic and theocratic character. On the contrary, it was decreed that the clergy should seize upon the Church, and should put themselves in its place. Speaking in its name, always presenting themselves as the sole depositary of its powers, the clergy will constitute its force, but at the same time will be the worm that eats away its strength, and the principal cause of its future decay.

History, I repeat, can show no example of a more complete transformation than that which took place in the government of the Christian Church about the time of Hadrian and Antoninus. What happened is what would happen in a club if the members abdicated in favour of the Committee, and the Committee in turn abdicated in favour of the President, in such

---

[1] Certain words of Jesus (Matt. xviii. 17—20) seemed to imply some such idea. But we must remember that only Matthew puts the word *ecclesia* into the mouth of Jesus.

a manner as to leave neither the members nor even the elders any deliberative voice, any influence, any control of funds, and to enable the President to say, "I alone am the club." The *presbyteri* (elders) or *episcopi* (superintending officers) very quickly became the only representatives of the Church, while, almost immediately afterwards, another still more important revolution was effected. Among the *presbyteri* or *episcopi*, there was one who, in virtue of habitually occupying the first seat, absorbed the powers of the rest, and became in a special way the *presbyteros* or *episcopos*. Public worship contributed largely to establish this unity. The eucharistic act could be performed only by a single person, and to that person gave a great importance.[1] This *episcopos* became, with surprising rapidity, the chief of the body of presbyters, and consequently of the whole Church. His *cathedra*, shaped like an arm-chair and standing out of the line, became a seat of honour, the token of primacy.[2] Each church has thenceforward only

---

[1] Letter of Irenæus to Victor, in Euseb. *II.E.* v. xxiv. 17.

[2] Ep. Petri ad Jac. 1. Ep. Clem. ad Jac. 2, 3, 6, 12, 16, 17, 19. Ignat. ad Philad. 3.

one chief *presbyteros,* who, to the exclusion of the rest, takes the name of *episcopos.*[1] By the side of this bishop we see deacons, widows, a council of presbyters:[2] but the important step has been taken; the bishop alone is the successor of the apostles; the faithful have entirely disappeared.[3] The apostolic authority, believed to be transmitted by the imposition of hands,[4] has destroyed the authority of the community.[5] The bishops of the different churches will afterwards enter into communication with one another, and will shape the universal Church into a species of oligarchy, which will hold meetings, will censure its own members, will decide questions of

---

[1] Conf. 1 Tim. iii. 1 et seq., v. 17—19, and especially Tit. i. 5, 6, 7. Conf. Phil. i. 1. In Clement of Rome (ch. 42) we have only priests and deacons.

[2] Πολύκαρπος καὶ οἱ σὺν αὐτῷ πρεσβύτεροι. Subscription of the Ep. of Polycarp.

[3] Προστάτης . . . προφήτης, θιασάρχης, ξυναγωγεὺς καὶ πάντα μόνος αὐτὸς ὤν. Lucian, *Peregr.* 11.

[4] ἐπίθεσις τῶν χειρῶν, which has nothing to do with χειροτονία.

[5] 1 Tim. iv. 14. Paul has given his orders to Timothy and Titus: these give their orders to the *presbyteri* or *episcopi* of the churches which they found. Tit. i. 5. These apostolic delegates have power over the *presbyteri.* 1 Tim. v. 17—19.

faith, and will, in and by itself, constitute a true sovereign power.

Before a hundred years had passed, the change was all but accomplished. When Hegesippus, in the second half of the second century, made his tour of Christendom, he found bishops everywhere: the only question which he raises is one of canonical succession: the living sentiment of churches no longer exists.[1] This revolution, however, was effected not without protest: the author of "The Shepherd," for instance, still attempts to maintain the primitive equality of the *presbyteri* against the growing authority of the bishops.[2] But the aristocratic tendency finally prevailed. On one side are the pastors, on the other the flock. The primitive equality is gone; to tell the truth, it had lasted only for a day. Henceforth the Church is only an instrument in the hands of those who direct it; and these directors derive their power, not from the community, but from a

---

[1] In Euseb. *H.E.* iv. xxii. 1—3.

[2] Πρωτοκαθεδρίται (Hermas, *Shepherd*, vis. iii. 9). Irenæus (in Euseb. *H.E.* v. xxiv. 14) stills calls the bishops of Rome *presbyteri* (οἱ πρεσβύτεροι, οἱ προστάντες τῆς ἐκκλησίας).

spiritual heredity,[1] a succession claiming to go back to the apostles in an uninterrupted line. We already feel that the representative system will never be, in any degree whatever, the law of the Christian Church.

It was the episcopate which, without any intervention of the civil power, without any support from police or courts of law, thus set order above liberty in a society which was originally founded on individual inspiration. And this is why the Ebionites, who had no bishops, had also no idea of Catholicity. At first sight, the work of Jesus did not seem likely to survive: it was a chaos. Founded upon a belief in the approaching end of the world, which the years as they rolled away could not but show to be mistaken, his congregation appeared to have nothing before it but to dissolve into anarchy. Freedom of prophecy, charismata, speaking with tongues, the inspiration of the individual—less than all this would have sufficed to reduce it to the proportions of an ephemeral congregation. Indivi-

---

[1] Διαδόχη.

dual inspiration creates, but at once destroys whatever it has created. After liberty must come order. The work of Jesus may be considered as safe from the day on which it was admitted that the Church had a power of its own, a power representing that of Jesus.[1] Thenceforth the Church dominates the individual, and if necessary casts him out from her bosom. Soon the Church, an unstable and fluctuating body, is personified in the elders: the powers of the Church become the powers of a clergy, who are the dispensers of the grace in which God communicates with the faithful. Inspiration passes over from the individual to the community. The Church becomes all in Christianity: one step more, and the Bishop becomes all in the Church. Obedience, first to the Church, at a later period to the Bishop, becomes the first of duties. novelty is the mark of error: to the Christian, schism will henceforth be the worst of crimes.

In one sense, we may say that this was a falling away—a lessening of the spontaneity which had

---

[1] Matt. xviii. 17—20.

been up to that time eminently creative. It was plain that ecclesiastical forms were about to absorb, to smother the work of Jesus, that all the free manifestations of the Christian life would soon be brought to a stand. Under the censure of the episcopate, speaking with tongues, prophecy, the creation of legends, the production of sacred books, will be failing and exhausted powers; the *charismata* will be reduced to official sacraments. Nevertheless, in another sense, this transformation was the essential condition of the energy of Christianity. And a concentration of powers became at once necessary when these churches grew to be tolerably numerous: the relations between these little pious societies were possible only so long as they had acknowledged representatives entitled to act for them. It is besides indisputable that, without the episcopate, churches brought into union for a moment by the recollection of Jesus, would soon have been scattered. Divergences of doctrine, differences in turn of mind, above all, rivalries, unsatisfied self-appreciations, would have produced their characteristic result of disunion and disintegration without end. Like

Mithraicism and so many other forms of belief to which it has not been given to conquer time, Christianity would have disappeared at the end of three or four hundred years. Democracy is sometimes eminently creative; but it is on condition that out of it are evolved conservative and aristocratic institutions which prevent the indefinite prolongation of the revolutionary fever.

This is the true miracle of nascent Christianity. It evolved order, hierarchy, authority, obedience from the voluntary subjection of wills: it organized the crowd; it disciplined anarchy. What effected this miracle, which astonishes us quite otherwise than pretended infringements of the laws of physical nature? It was the spirit of Jesus, strongly grafted into his disciples; the spirit of sweetness, of self-abnegation, of forgetfulness of the present; that unique pursuit of inward joys which kills ambition; that preference boldly given to childhood; those words perpetually repeated as from the lips of Jesus, "And whosoever will be chief among you, let him be your servant." The impression left by the apostles contributed hardly less to the same result. The apostles and their immediate delegates had undisputed power over the Church. Now, the episcopate was held to be the heir of apostolic powers.[1] The apostles lived and governed after their death. The idea that the president of the Church derives his authority from the members of the Church who have elected him, never once appears in the literature of this age. Thus, in virtue of the supernatural origin of its power, the Church avoids whatever is frail and transitory in all delegated authority. Legislative and executive authority may spring from the multitude; but sacraments, the dispensations of heavenly grace, have nothing in common with universal suffrage. Such privileges descend from heaven, or, to adopt the Christian formula, from Jesus Christ, the fountain of all grace and all good.

But, to speak with perfect accuracy, the bishop had never been elected by the whole community. The nomination by the Holy Spirit,[2] that is to say, the secret employment of electoral manœuvres, ex-

---

[1] Clem. Rom. *Ep.* i. c. 42, 44.
[2] Clem. Alex. *Quis dives salvetur*, 42.

cusable on the supposition of an extreme simplicity of mind, sufficed for the spontaneous enthusiasm of the first churches. When the apostolic age had passed away, and it was necessary that an ecclesiastical decision should supply the place of that kind of divine right which was supposed to belong to the apostles and their immediate disciples,[1] the elders chose their president from among themselves, and offered him to the acclamations of the people.[2] As this choice was never made without some previous collection of opinions, the acclamation, or rather the vote by show of hands,[3] was in fact only a formality; but it was enough to preserve the recollection of the evangelical ideal, according to which the spirit of Jesus really resided in the whole community.[4] The election of deacons was in like manner a double

---

[1] Tit. i. 5; 1 Tim. v. 22. Clem. Alex. *Quis dives salvetur*, 42.

[2] Clem. Rom. *Ep.* i. ch. 44.

[3] χειροτονία. In Acts xiv. 23, and 2 Cor. viii. 19, as indeed in many passages of Greek classical authors, χειροτονεῖν has, by extension, the sense of "to choose," without implying the actual assemblage and show of hands. Conf. *Const. Apost.* vii. 31.

[4] Matt. xviii. 17—20.

process. The nomination was made by the bishop, but the approbation of the community was necessary to the validity of the choice.¹ A general law of the Church is, that the inferior never elects his superior. This it is which in our own day, in the midst of the absolutely contrary tendency of modern democracy, endows the Church with so great an energy of reaction.

This movement towards hierarchy and episcopacy was especially felt in the churches of Paul. The Jewish-Christian churches, on a lower level of vitality, remained synagogues, and did not so decisively tend to clericalism. On this account it was that arguments on behalf of the doctrine which it was desired to inculcate were conveyed in writings ascribed to Paul. An Epistle of St. Paul was an authority of extraordinary weight. Many passages in his authentic letters already made much of the hierarchy, of respect for the authority of elders. But to furnish arguments of a still more decisive kind, three short letters, supposed to be written by Paul to his disci-

---

¹ *Const. Apost.* iii. 15, vii. 31.

ples Timothy and Titus, were put forth. The author of these apocryphal writings had not the Acts of the Apostles in his hands; he had only a vague knowledge of the apostolical journeys of Paul,[1] and was unacquainted with their details. As very few persons had more accurate notions on the subject than himself, this did not compromise him much; while, again, the critical faculty was at that time so utterly wanting, that no one dreamed of deciding any subject of debate by a comparison of documents.

These three short letters, evidently the work of one pen and probably composed at Rome,[2] are an early treatise on ecclesiastical duties, a first sketch of false decretals, a code of law for the use of churchmen.[3] The episcopate is a great thing indeed.[4] The bishop is, as it were, a model of perfection proposed to his subordinates.[5] He must therefore be blameless

---

[1] I have shown this in my *St. Paul*, Introd. pp. xxiii—lii.

[2] Vid. *St. Paul*, Introd. pp. li, lii.

[3] "In ordinatione ecclesiasticæ disciplinæ sanctificatæ sunt." Canon of Muratori, L 61, 62.

[4] 1 Tim. iii.; Tit. i. The bishop is called $\theta\epsilon o\hat{v}$ $o\mathit{i}\kappa o\nu\acute{o}\mu o s$, Tit. i. 7.

[5] 1 Tim. iv. 12; Tit. ii. 7, 8.

in the eyes both of the faithful and of strangers. His family must be grave like himself. If any man knows not how to rule his own household, how shall he govern the Church of God? Orthodox above all, attached to the true faith, the sworn enemy of error, the bishop exhorts, instructs. For such functions it is not right to choose either a new convert, lest his too rapid elevation lead him astray, or a man capable of passionate anger, or one who exercises a profession which is not in good repute. Even unbelievers ought to respect the bishop, and to have nothing to allege against him.

Thanks to the Church of Rome, the religion of Jesus thus acquired a certain solidity and consistency. The great danger of Gnosticism, which threatened to divide Christendom into innumerable sects, was averted. The phrase "Catholic Church"[1] breaks upon us from all sides at once, as the name of the great communion which is destined thence-

---

[1] ἐκκλησία καθολική. Letter of the Church of Smyrna on the martyrdom of Polycarp, title, § 8, 16. Celsus, in Origen, v. 59, ἡ μεγάλη ἐκκλησία. Conf. Canon of Muratori, L 55, 57, 61, 62, 66, 69.

forth to come down the ages in unbroken unity. And the character of this catholicity is already sufficiently visible. The Montanists are regarded as sectaries; the Marcionites are convicted of falsifying apostolical doctrine; the different Gnostic schools are more and more repelled from the bosom of the general Church. There is, then, something which is neither Montanism, nor Marcionism, nor Gnosticism—unsectarian Christianity, the Christianity of the majority of bishops, resisting and using all the sects, having, if you will, none but negative characteristics, but by those very negative characteristics preserved from pietistic aberrations and dissolvent rationalism. Christianity, like every other party that wishes to live, disciplines itself, cuts off its own excesses. It joins to an exalted mysticism a fund of good sense and moderation which will be fatal to millenarianism, charismata, speaking with tongues, all the primitive spiritual phenomena. A handful of fanatics, such as the Montanists, affronting martyrdom, discouraging penitence, condemning marriage— these are not the Church. The *juste milieu* triumphs. it will not be given to radicals of any kind to destroy the work of Jesus. The Church is everybody's affair, not the privilege of an aristocracy. The pietist aristocracy of the Phrygian sects, the speculative aristocracy of the Gnostics, must alike submit to the rejection of their claims.

In the midst of the enormous variety of opinions of which the first Christian century is full, a fixed point thus constitutes itself, the opinion of Catholicity. To convict the heretic, it is not necessary to argue with him. It is enough to prove to him that he is not in communion with the Catholic Church, with the great Churches which can show an undisputed succession of bishops from the apostles.[1] *Quod semper quod ubique* becomes the absolute rule of truth. The argument of prescription, to which Tertullian is afterwards to give so eloquent a force, sums up all the Catholic controversy. To prove to any one that he is an innovator, a late comer in theology, is to prove that he is wrong. An insufficient rule, after all: for, by a singular irony of fate, the very doctor who, in so imperious a way, drew out this method of refutation, himself died a heretic.

---

[1] Iren. iii. iv. 1. Tertull. *Præscr.* 36.

Correspondence between churches soon became customary.[1] The circular letters of the heads of the great Churches, read on Sunday in the assembly of the faithful, were in some sort a continuation of the apostolical literature. The ecclesiastical province, implying the presidency of the great Churches, appeared in germ. The church, like the synagogue and the mosque, is a thing that essentially belongs to the city. Christianity, like Judaism and Islamism, is to be a religion of towns. The final resistance which it has to encounter will come from the countryman, the *paganus*. The rural Christians, who were very few in number, no doubt frequented the church of the neighbouring town.[2] The Roman *municipium* thus gave local limits to the Church. As the country and the small towns received the gospel from the cities, they also received from them their clergy, who were always subordinate to the bishop of the great town. Thus among the towns, the *civitas*, the great town, alone has a real church,

---

[1] We may recal the discussion on the subject of Montanism, the observance of Easter, &c. Above all, see Euseb. *H.E.* v. 25.

[2] Justin. *Apol.* i. 67.

168   ROME, THE CAPITAL OF

with an *episcopos;* the small town remains in ecclesiastical dependence upon the great one.[1] This primacy of great towns was a fact of capital importance. The great town once converted, the small town and the country followed the movement. The diocese[2] was thus the original unit of the Christian organization. As to the ecclesiastical province, it answered in general to the Roman province; the divisions set up by the worship of Rome and of Augustus, were here the secret law which determined all. The towns which had a *flamen*, or *archiereus*, are those which at a later time had an archbishop; the *flamen civitatis*, whose special charge was the worship of the Lares, became the bishop; after the third century, he possesses the civil and political powers in the *civitas*, to which the bishop will succeed.[3] The *flamen*, in a word, occupied in the city the same rank as the bishop afterwards did

---

[1] Council of Ancyra (315).

[2] The word παροικία is almost synonymous with church or diocese. Title of the Letter of the Church of Smyrna on the martyrdom of Polycarp. Iren. in Euseb. *H. E.* v. xxiv. 14; compare 9, and i. i. 1; iii. xxviii. 3; iv. xv. 2; v. v. 8; xxiii. 2; vi. xi. 1.

[3] In the Acts of the Martyrs, the flamen is often the persecutor.

in the diocese.[1] Thus it comes to pass that the ecclesiastical geography of a country is almost identical with its geography in the Roman period. The map of bishoprics and archbishoprics is that of the ancient *civitates*, in their order of political subordination. The Empire was, as it were, the mould in which the new religion took shape. The inner framework, the limits, the hierarchical divisions of the Church, were those of the Empire. There is hardly any difference to be perceived between the old rolls of the Roman administration and the registers of the Church in the middle ages, or even in our own day.

Thus these great organisms, which have become so essential a part of the moral and political life of the European peoples, were all created by the simple and sincere men whose faith has become inseparable from the moral culture of humanity. Under Marcus Aurelius, the episcopate is completely ripe: the Papacy exists in germ. Ecumenical Councils were not yet possible; only the

---

[1] Renier and Allmer, *Revue Épigr.* No. 4, p. 62.

Christian Empire could permit these great assemblies: but the Provincial Synod was brought to bear upon the Montanist and the Paschal controversies: the presidency of the Bishop of the capital of the province was admitted without dispute.

A work which well shows the rapid progress of this inner movement towards the constitution, or, let us rather say, the exaggeration of hierarchical authority, is the correspondence ascribed to St. Ignatius, to which the letter of St. Polycarp is possibly an appendix.[1] Who better than these two great bishops and martyrs, whose memory was everywhere held in reverence, could counsel the faithful to submission and order?

"Obey the Bishop as Jesus Christ obeyed the Father, and the body of Presbyters as the Apostles: revere the deacons as you would the very commandment of God. Let no one do anything in whatever

---

[1] The objections to the authenticity of these Epistles are not lessened by bringing down the martyrdom of Ignatius to the time of Hadrian or of Antoninus, as Harnack (*Die Zeit des Ignatius*, Leipzig, 1878) has lately done. It is in their style and turn of thought that the apocryphal character of these letters shows itself.

concerns the Church without the Bishop. As regards the Eucharist, that must be held to be good which is administered by the Bishop, or by him to whom the Bishop has entrusted it. Wherever the Bishop is visible, there let the people be: in the same way as where Jesus Christ is, there is the Church Catholic. Without the Bishop it is not allowed either to baptize or to celebrate the agapé; on the contrary, the approbation of the Bishop is the mark of what is well pleasing to God, the firm and sure rule to follow in practice."[1] "It is proper, then, that you should agree with the opinion of the Bishop, as you do. For your venerable body of presbyters, worthy of God, stands in the same relation to the Bishop as do the strings to the lyre. Wherefore in your agreement and concordant love Jesus Christ is sung."[2]

This was written about the year 160 or 170. A purely ecclesiastical piety took the place of the ancient ardour which for more than a hundred years had been kindled by the recollection of Jesus. Or-

---

[1] Ignat. *Ep. ad Smyrn.* 8. Conf. *Ep. ad Philad.* 1.

[2] Ignat. *Ep. ad Eph.* 4.

thodoxy is now the chief good: docility is salvation: the old man must bend before the bishop, even if he be young.[1] It was thus that, by pushing to an extreme the principles of Paul, men arrived at ideas which would have revolted Paul. Would he, who was unwilling to listen for a moment to salvation by works, ever have admitted that a man could be saved by simple submission to his superiors?

II.

Rome was the place in which this great idea of Catholicity was worked out. More and more every day it became the capital of Christianity, and took the place of Jerusalem as the religious centre of humanity. Its Church claimed a precedence over others which was generally recognized.[2] All the doubtful questions which agitated the Christian con-

---

[1] See especially the reputed Epistle of Ignatius to Polycarp, and the Epistle of Polycarp himself. Ignat. *ad Eph.* 3, 5; *ad Magn.* 3—7, 13; *ad Trall.* 2, 3, 12; *ad Philad.* 1—4, 7, 8; *ad Smyrn.* 8, 9; *ad Polyc.* 6.

[2] Iren. iii. iii. Tertull. *Præscr.* 21, 36. Cyprian, *Ep.* 52, 55 (ecclesiam principalem unde unitas sacerdotum exorta est), 67, 71, 75 (Firmilian).

science came to Rome to ask for arbitration, if not decision. Men argued, certainly not in a very logical way, that as Christ had made Cephas the corner-stone of his Church, the privilege ought to be inherited by his successors. By an unequalled *tour de force*, the Church of Rome had succeeded in giving itself the name of the Church of Paul also. A new and equally mythical duality replaced that of Romulus and Remus. The Bishop of Rome became the Bishop of bishops, he who admonished all others. Rome proclaims her right—a dangerous right—of excommunicating those who do not walk step by step with her. The poor Artemonites—a kind of Arians before Arius—have great reason to complain of the injustice of fate, which has branded them as heretics, although up to the time of Victor the whole Church of Rome was of one mind with them.[1] From that time forth, the Church of Rome put herself above history. At the end of the second century we can already recognize, by signs which it is impossible to mistake, the spirit which in 1870 will proclaim the infallibility of the Pope. The writing

---

[1] Euseb. *H. E.* v. xxviii. 3.

of which the fragment known as the Canon of Muratori formed a part, and which was produced at Rome about the year 180 A.D., shows us Rome already defining the canon of Scripture, alleging the martyrdom of Peter as the foundation of Catholicity, repudiating Montanism and Gnosticism alike. Irenæus refutes all heresies by reference to the belief of this Church, "the greatest, the oldest, the most illustrious, which possesses, in virtue of an unbroken succession, the true tradition of the apostles Peter and Paul, and to which, because of its Primacy, all the rest of the Church ought to have recourse."[1]

A material cause greatly contributed to the preeminence which all the churches recognized as belonging to the Church of Rome. This Church was extremely rich: its wealth, ably administered, furnished funds to other churches, both for purposes of charity and the propagation of the faith. Confessors condemned to labour in the mines received help from Rome.[2] There, in some sort, was the

---

[1] Irenæus, iii. iii. 2.

[2] Dionys. of Corinth, in Euseb. *H.E.* iv. xxiii. 9, 10. Conf. Dionys. of Alex. in Euseb. *H. E.* vii. v. 2. Basil. *Ep.* 220, and the reflection of Euseb. *H.E.* iv. xxiii. 9.

common treasury of Christianity. The Sunday's collection, a constant practice of the Church of Rome, was in all likelihood already established. A wonderful spirit of direction animated this little community, to which Judea, Greece, Latium, seemed, in view of a prodigious future, to have contributed the most various gifts. While Jewish Monotheism furnished the immovable base of the new foundation, and Greece continued in Gnosticism her work of free speculation, Rome applied herself with astonishing success to the task of government. Every kind of authority, every kind of artifice, served her to that end. Policy never recoils from fraud, and policy had already found a home in the most secret councils of the Church of Rome. The vein of apocryphal literature was constantly worked; writings published under the guarantee of Rome, and ascribed sometimes to apostles, sometimes to apostolical personages such as Clement and Hermas, were received with confiding faith throughout the Christian world.

This precedence of the Church of Rome only became more marked in the third century. The

Bishops of Rome showed a rare ability, in avoiding theological questions, while they kept themselves to the front in all matters of organization and administration. The tradition of the Roman Church passes for the most ancient of all.[1] Cornelius takes the first place in the affair of Novatianism: we see him, in especial, depriving Italian bishops and nominating their successors.[2] Rome was also the central authority of the African churches.[3]

And already this authority was becoming overweening. We see this in the Paschal controversy. The question was a much graver one than we should now be disposed to believe. In the earliest times, all Christians continued to make the Jewish Passover their chief festival. They celebrated it on the same day as the Jews, the 14th of Nisan, no matter in what part of the week that day might fall. Convinced, in accordance with the account of all ancient Gospels, that Jesus on the eve of his death had eaten

---

[1] εὐξάμενος τὴν ἀρχαιοτάτην Ῥωμαίων ἐκκλησίαν ἰδεῖν. Origen, in Euseb. *H.E.* vi. xiv. 10.

[2] Letter of Cornelius, in Euseb. *H.E.* vi. xliii. 8, 10

[3] Tertull. *Præscr.* 21. Cyprian, *Ep.* 52, 55, 71, 75 (Firmilian).

the Passover with his disciples, they regarded such a solemnity as much more a commemoration of the Supper than a memorial of the Resurrection. But in proportion as Christianity more and more separated itself from Judaism, this way of looking at the matter became less easy. First, a new tradition gained currency, to the effect that Jesus before his death had not eaten the Passover, but had died on the very day of the Passover, thus substituting himself for the Paschal Lamb. But beyond this, a purely Jewish festival wounded the Christian conscience, especially in the Pauline churches. The great Christian festival was the Resurrection of Jesus, which in any case must have taken place on the Sunday after the Jewish Passover. In conformity with this idea, men celebrated the festival of Easter on the Sunday which followed the Friday next after the 14th of Nisan.

At Rome this custom prevailed, at least subsequently to the pontificates of Xystus and Telesphorus (about the year 126). In Asia, opinion was much divided. Conservatives, such as Polycarp, Melito and all the older school, adhered to the ancient

Jewish practice, as in conformity with the first Gospels and the usage of the apostles John and Philip. This was the object of the journey to Rome which Polycarp undertook about the year 154, in the papacy of Anicetus. The meeting between Polycarp and Anicetus was very friendly. The discussion on certain points appears to have been somewhat sharp, but an understanding was arrived at. Polycarp could not persuade Anicetus to give up a usage which had been that of preceding Bishops of Rome. Anicetus, on the other side, held his hand when Polycarp informed him that he derived his rule from John and the other apostles, with whom, he alleged, he had lived on a footing of familiarity. The two religious chiefs remained in full communion with one another: Anicetus even did honour to Polycarp in an almost unexampled way. He requested Polycarp, in the assembly of the faithful at Rome, to pronounce for him, and in his presence, the words of eucharistic consecration.[1] These zealous men

---

[1] Irenæus, letter to Victor, loc. cit. The verb $\pi\alpha\rho\epsilon\chi\omega\rho\eta\sigma\epsilon$, implying the giving up of a right, cannot mean that Anicetus simply gave the consecrated bread and wine to Polycarp.

were animated by too noble a feeling to allow them to base unity of heart upon uniformity of external rites and observances.

Unfortunately, at a later period Rome addressed herself with great obstinacy to the task of making her usage universal. About the year 196, the question arose in a more decisive form than ever.[1] The churches of Asia persisted in their old practice: Rome, always eager for unity, desired to assimilate it to her own. On the invitation of Pope Victor,[2] meetings of bishops were held, a vast correspondence was exchanged. But the bishops of Asia, strong in the traditions of two apostles and so many illustrious men, would not yield. Polycrates, the aged Bishop of Ephesus, wrote in their name a somewhat stern letter to Victor and the Church of Rome.[3] The incredible design which the rather severe terms of this epistle

---

[1] Euseb. *H.E.* v. xxiii. xxiv. xxv. Jerome, *Chron.* Schœne, pp. 174, 177. *De viris ill.* ch. 35, 43—45. Anatolius, in Bucherius, *De Cycl.* pp. 443 et seq. Labbe's Councils, i. 600. Photius, ch. 120.

[2] Polycrates, in Euseb. *H.E.* v. xxiv. 8.

[3] Euseb. *H.E.* v. xxiv. 2 et seq. Conf. iii. xxxi. 3.

suggested to the mind of Victor, is a sufficient proof that the Papacy was already born, and well born. He claimed the right to excommunicate, to separate from the universal Church, its most illustrious province, because it did not make its traditions bend before the Roman discipline. He published a decree by which the churches of Asia were put under the ban of the Christian community.[1] But the other bishops set themselves against this violent measure, and recalled Victor to charity.[2] Irenæus of Lyons, in particular, who, under the prevailing influences of the region to which he had migrated, had accepted for himself and his Gaulish churches the Western custom, could not endure the thought that the mother churches of Asia, to which he felt himself attached by the tenderest ties, should be separated from the body of the universal Church. He energetically dissuaded Victor from excommunicating churches which adhered to the tradition of their fathers, and recalled to his mind the example of his more tolerant predecessors. This act of singular

---

[1] στηλιτεύει διὰ γραμμάτων, ἀκοινωνήτους ἀνακηρύττων.

[2] Eusebius had their letters in his possession.

good sense prevented the schism of East and West from taking place in the second century. Irenæus wrote to bishops in every direction; and the churches of Asia were left free to do as they would.

In one sense, the procedure which this debate involved was more important than the debate itself. A consequence of the difference was, that the Church was led to entertain a clearer conception of its own organization. And, in the first place, it was evident that the laity no longer counted for anything. Bishops alone interfere, give advice. They assemble in provincial synods, presided over by the bishop of the capital of the province,[1]—the archbishop of the future,—sometimes by the oldest among them. The synodical assembly resolves upon a letter which is despatched to other churches. It is a kind of experiment in federative organization, an attempt to resolve difficulties by means of provincial assemblies, presided over by bishops, and afterwards communicating with one another. At a later period, the records of this great debate will be searched with a

---

[1] Thus the Bishop of Cæsarea took precedence of the Bishop of Jerusalem.

view of finding precedents as to questions of the presidency of synods, and of ecclesiastical hierarchy in general. Among all churches, that of Rome appears to possess a special right of initiative. But this initiative was far from being synonymous with infallibility; for Eusebius declares that he had read letters in which bishops strongly blamed Victor's conduct.[1]

III.

Authority loves authority: the possessors of authority of every kind hold out a hand to one another. Men as conservative as were the heads of the Church of Rome must have felt a strong temptation towards reconciliation with the power of the State, which they admitted to be often exerted for good. This tendency had been noticeable from the earliest days of Christianity. Jesus himself had laid down the rule. For him, the image and superscription on the coin were the ultimate criterion of legitimate power, a criterion which left no room for further inquiry. While Nero was upon the throne, Paul wrote: "Let

---

[1] Euseb. *H. E.* v. xxiv. 10: πληκτικώτερον καθαπτομένων τοῦ Βίκτορος. Conf. Socrat. v. 22.

every soul be subject unto the higher powers. For there is no power but of God: the powers that be are ordained of God. Whosoever, therefore, resisteth the power, resisteth the ordinance of God. . . . Wilt thou, then, not be afraid of the power? Do that which is good, and thou shalt have praise of the same; for he is the minister of God to thee for good. But if thou do that which is evil, be afraid; for he beareth not the sword in vain: for he is the minister of God, a revenger to execute wrath upon him that doeth evil. Wherefore ye must needs be subject, not only for wrath, but for conscience' sake. For for this cause pay ye tribute also; for they are God's ministers,[1] attending continually upon this very thing."[2]

Some years afterwards, Peter, or whoever wrote in his name the work known as his First Epistle, expresses himself in almost identical terms: "Submit yourselves to every ordinance of man for the Lord's sake, whether it be to the king as supreme, or unto governors, as unto them that are sent by

---

[1] Λειτουργοὶ θεοῦ. [2] Rom. xiii. 1—7; conf. Tit. iii. 1.

him for the punishment of evil-doers, and for the praise of them that do well."[1] In the same way, Clement is a subject of the Roman Empire, whose loyalty cannot be surpassed. The submission which is due to bishops and elders, the Christian ought to pay to the powers of the world. At the very moment of Nero's most diabolical atrocities, we have just heard Peter and Paul declare that the monster's power came from God. Clement, at the time when Domitian was raging most cruelly against the Church and the human race, holds him likewise to be the lieutenant of God. In that part of his Epistle which has been recently recovered, he thus speaks:[2] "It is Thou, Master Supreme, who by Thy great and unspeakable power hast given to our sovereigns, and to those who rule us upon earth, the power of royalty, that we, knowing the glory and the honour which Thou hast imparted to them, may be submissive to them, and in no wise run counter to Thy will. Give Thou to them, O Lord, health, peace, concord, stability, that they may exercise without

---

[1] 1 Pet. ii. 13 et seq.   [2] Clem. Rom. *Ad Cor.* ch. 61.

hindrance the sovereignty which Thou hast confided to them. . . . . Direct, Lord, their will according to that which is good and well-pleasing in Thy sight, in order that, piously exercising in peace and mildness the power which Thou hast given them, they may find Thee propitious."

Lastly, a characteristic of St. Luke—and you know that in my view there is a connection between St. Luke and the spirit of the Church of Rome—is his respect for the imperial authority, and the precautions which he takes not to offend it. The author of the Acts avoids whatever might present the Romans in the light of enemies of Christianity. On the contrary, he tries to show that in many cases they defended St. Paul and the Christians against the Jews.[1] He never utters a word that could be offensive to the civil magistrate. He loves to show how the Roman functionaries were favourable to the new sect, and sometimes even joined it;[2] how equitable Roman justice is, and how superior to the

---

[1] Acts xxiv. 7, 17, xxv. 9, 16, 25, xxviii. 17, 18.
[2] The centurion Cornelius, the proconsul Paulus.

passions of merely local authorities.[1] He insists upon the advantage which Paul derived from his Roman citizenship.[2] If he closes his narrative with the arrival of Paul in Rome, it is possibly in order to avoid the necessity of recounting the atrocities of Nero. Luke nowhere allows that the Christians were compromised before the law. If Paul had not appealed to the Emperor, he "might have been set at liberty." A legal *arrière pensée*, in full accord with the age of Trajan, pre-occupies him: he wishes to create precedents, to show that there is no ground for persecuting those whom Roman tribunals have so often acquitted.

It must be confessed that there were in other parts of the Empire fanatics who fully shared the anger of the Jews, and dreamed of the destruction of the idolatrous city, which they identified with Babylon. Such were the authors of Apocalypses and Sibylline verses. But the faithful of the great Churches entertained very different sentiments. In

---

[1] Acts xiii. 7 et seq., xviii. 12 et seq., xix. 35 et seq., xxiv. 7, 17, xxv. 9, 16, 25, xxvii. 2, xxviii. 17, 18.

[2] Acts xvi. 37 et seq., xxii. 26 et seq.

the year 70, the Church of Jerusalem, yielding to a feeling which was more Christian than patriotic, abandoned the revolutionary city, and departed to seek peace beyond the Jordan. In the revolt of Barchochbas, the separation was still more marked. Not a single Christian was found to take part in that attempt of a blind despair. Justin Martyr, in his Apologies, never contends against the principle of the Empire: what he wants is, that the Empire should examine Christian doctrine, should approve it, should in some sort countersign it, and should condemn those who calumniate it.[1] The first doctor of the age of Marcus Aurelius, Melito, Bishop of Sardes, makes still more decisive advances to the State, and applies himself to show that Christianity has that in it which should recommend it to the favour of a true Roman. In his treatise on Truth, preserved in a Syriac version,[2] Melito expresses himself as a Bishop of the fourth century might do, explaining to one Theodorus that

---

[1] Justin Martyr, *Apol.* ii. 14.
[2] Cureton, *Spicil. Syr.* pp. 48 et seq.

his first duty is to use his authority to procure the triumph of truth, without, alas! telling us by what tokens truth is to be recognized. Let the Empire become Christian, and the persecuted of the present time will find the interference of the State in the domain of conscience perfectly legitimate. In other passages, Melito is still more complaisant to the powers that be.

"A thing that has never before been seen," says he, "is that the race of pious men is now persecuted, hunted through Asia in virtue of new edicts.[1] Impudent sycophants and lovers of other men's goods, making a pretext of existing decrees, practise robbery publicly, watching day and night to lay hold of those who have done no wrong. . . . . If these things are being done by thy order, let it be well. For a just king cannot, under any circumstances, devise what is unjust. And we willingly accept such a death as the lot which we have deserved. One request we make unto thee, that after having thine own self examined those

---

[1] Fragment in Euseb. *H. E.* iv. xxvi. 1, 7 et seq.

who are brought before thee as actors in rebellion, thou wouldst be pleased to judge whether they deserve death, or if they are not rather worthy to live in peace, under the protection of the law. . . . . For our philosophy first had its birth among the barbarians, but the fact that the moment at which it began to flourish among the people of thy states coincided with the great reign of Augustus, thy ancestor, was a happy augury for the Empire. For from this time the Roman power grew into something great and splendid, of which thou, with thy son,[1] art and shalt be the heir, the subject of our prayers, if only thou art willing to protect this philosophy, which has been in some sort the foster-sister of the Empire, since it was born with its founder, and has been honoured by thine ancestors on an equality with other worships. And it is the greatest proof that our doctrine has been destined to flourish, side by side with the progress of thy glorious Empire, that from the time of its appearance all has wonderfully succeeded with you. Nero

---

[1] These words are addressed to Marcus Aurelius. The son who is spoken of is Commodus.

and Domitian only, deceived by certain calumnious men, showed ill-will towards our religion; and these calumnies, as is usually the case, were afterwards accepted without examination. But their error has been corrected by thy pious fathers,[1] who in frequent rescripts have repressed the zeal of those who wished to adopt rigorous means against us...... As to thyself, who cherishest the same feelings towards us as they, only in a still more philanthropic and philosophical way, we are confident that thou wilt do as we ask of thee."

The system of the Apologists, so warmly maintained by Tertullian,[2] according to which the good Emperors favoured Christianity and the bad Emperors persecuted it, was already, as we see, fully developed. Born together, Christianity and Rome had together grown great and prospered. Their interests, their sufferings, their fortune, their future, all were in common.[3] The Apologists were advo-

---

[1] Hadrian and Antoninus Pius.

[2] Tertull. *Apol.* 5. Conf. *Apol.* 21.

[3] The author of the Sibylline poem, contained in Books xi.—xiv., expresses the same idea; xii. 30—36, 230—235.

cates, and advocates of all kinds are alike. They have arguments for every situation and for every taste. Almost 150 years will roll away before these honeyed and not too sincere invitations find a hearing. But the very fact that in the reign of Marcus Aurelius they suggest themselves to the mind of one of the most enlightened chiefs of the Church, is a prognostic of the future. Christianity and the Empire will be reconciled: they are formed for one another. The shade of Melito will thrill with joy when the Empire becomes Christian, and the Emperor takes in hand the cause of "the truth."

In this way the Church made more than one step towards the Empire. For politeness' sake, no doubt, but also as a legitimate deduction from his principles, Melito does not admit that an Emperor can give an unjust order. Men were willing to have it believed, though contrary to all truth, that certain Emperors had not been absolutely opposed to Christianity: they loved to tell how Tiberius had proposed to the Senate to place Jesus among the gods, and how it was the Senate that had been unwilling.[1]

---

[1] Tertull. *Apol.* 5.

The decided preference shown by Christianity for powers that be, whenever it can hope to share their favour, is already plain enough. A violent attempt is made to show, in despite of facts, that Hadrian and Antoninus endeavoured to repair the evil done by Nero and Domitian. Tertullian and his generation will say the same kind of thing of Marcus Aurelius.[1] Tertullian, it is true, will have his doubts as to whether it is possible to be Cæsar and Christian at once; but a century afterwards, this incompatibility will strike no one; and Constantine will prove how great was the sagacity of Melito of Sardes when, a century and a half beforehand, he foresaw, across so many proconsular persecutions, the possibility of a Christian empire.

The hatred between Christianity and the Empire was the hatred of those who are some day to become lovers. Under the Severi, the language of the Church remained what it had been under the Antonines, plaintive and tender. The Apologists parade a kind of legitimism: they claim for the Church that it has always, from the first, recognized the

---

[1] Tertull. *Apol.* 5.

true Emperor. "There have never been among us," says Tertullian, "partizans of Cassius, partizans of Albinus, partizans of Niger."[1] A slight illusion! Certainly the revolt of Avidius Cassius against Marcus Aurelius was a political crime, in which the Christians did well to take no part. As to Severus, Albinus and Niger, success was the only thing which gave one a preference over the rest; and the Church, in attaching itself to Severus, can claim no other merit than that of adroitly divining which would turn out strongest. This pretended regard for legitimacy was at bottom only the worship of accomplished fact. St. Paul's principle was bearing fruit. All power comes from God: he who holds the sword, holds it of God for good.

This correct attitude towards secular powers was due to external necessities quite as much as to the principles which the Church had received from its founders. The Church was already a powerful association: it was essentially conservative: it had need of order and legal guarantees. This is admirably

---

[1] Tertull. *Ad Scap.* 3.

seen in the affair of Paul of Samosata, Bishop of Antioch under Aurelian.[1] Even at this period the Bishop of Antioch might be regarded as a powerful personage. The wealth of the Church was in his hands: a crowd of people lived upon his favour. Paul was a brilliant man, little inclined to mysticism, worldly, a secular "grand seigneur," trying to make Christianity acceptable to men of the world and people in authority. The pietists, as might be expected, found out that he was a heretic, and procured his deprivation. Paul resisted, and refused to leave his episcopal palace. This is the point at which the haughtiest sects are vulnerable: they hold property; and how can a question of property or of usufruct be determined except by the civil power? Aurelian, about this time, came to Antioch: the question was referred to him; and the world saw the strange sight of an unbelieving and persecuting sovereign called upon to decide who was the true Bishop. Aurelian, under these circumstances, gave proof of the possession of a layman's good

---

[1] Euseb. *H.E.* vii. 36.

sense to a very remarkable degree. He had the correspondence of the two Bishops brought to him; noticed which was in communion with Rome and Italy, and decided that *he* was the true Bishop of Antioch. Aurelian's theological reasoning in this case is open to many objections; but two things became evident, first that Christianity could no longer live without the Empire, and next that the Empire could do nothing better than adopt Christianity as its religion. The world wanted a religion of congregations, of churches, of synagogues, of chapels —a religion the essence of whose worship should be union, association, fraternity. All these conditions Christianity fulfilled. Its admirable worship, its pure morality, its wisely organized clergy, made the future its own.

More than once in the third century this historical necessity all but realized itself. This was especially the case under those Syrian Emperors whose foreign birth and low origin freed them from the influence of prejudice, and who, in spite of their vices, inaugurated a breadth of ideas and a toleration which up to that time had been unknown. These Syrian women of Emesa, Julia Domna, Julia Maesa, Julia Mammea, Julia Soemia, young, intelligent, hardy and almost utopian in conception, held back by no social tradition or convention, stop at nothing: they do what no Roman woman has ever dared to do; they enter the Senate, take part in its deliberations, actually govern the Empire, dream of Semiramis and Nitocris. The Roman worship is in their eyes cold and unmeaning: not being attached to it by any ancestral ties, and feeling their religious imagination more in harmony with Christianity than with Italian paganism, these women take pleasure in stories of gods who visit the earth. Philostratus enchants them with his Apollonius: possibly they may have had secret affinities with Christianity in more directions than one. It is true that Heliogabalus was a madman; yet, nevertheless, his wild dream of a central monotheistic worship established at Rome, and absorbing all other worships, showed that the narrow circle of ideas in which the Antonines had lived was broken through. Alexander Severus went further: he had a fellow-feeling with the Christians: not content with granting them liberty, he showed a touching eclecticism when he placed the image of Jesus in his *lararium*. Peace seemed to be concluded, not, as in the time of Constantine, by the defeat of one of the opposing parties, but by a broad reconciliation. The same thing took place again under Philip the Arabian, in the East under Zenobia, and in general under the Emperors whom foreign birth excluded from the circle of Roman patriotism.

The struggle became one of life and death when those great reformers, Diocletian and Maximian, animated by the ancient spirit, imagined that they could give a fresh life to the Roman Empire, while still keeping within the narrow round of Roman ideas. The Church triumphed in its martyrs: the Roman pride gave way: Constantine saw the inner force of the Church: the populations of Asia Minor, of Syria, of Thrace, of Macedonia—in a word, of the Eastern part of the Empire, were already more than half Christian. The mother of Constantine, who had been a servant-maid in an inn at Nicomedia, held up before his eyes the image of an Eastern Empire, with its centre about Nicæa or Nicomedia, whose strength should lie in the bishops, and in those masses of the poor, affiliated to the Church, who in the large towns directed public opinion. Constantine made the Empire Christian. When we look at this from the point of view of the West, we are astonished, for there the Christians were as yet only a weak minority. But in the East, the policy of Constantine was not only natural, but compelled by circumstance.

Strange to say, it was from this policy that the city of Rome received the heaviest blow that ever fell upon it. Christianity succeeded with Constantine, but it was Eastern Christianity. In building a new Rome on the Bosporus, Constantine reduced old Rome to the position of being capital of the West only. The cataclysms that followed, the invasions of barbarians which spared Constantinople to fall with their full weight upon Rome, compelled the ancient metropolis of the world to play a narrow, often a humble part. That Roman primacy, which is so brilliant a fact in the second and third century, ceases to exist as soon as the East has a separate existence and a separate capital. Constantine is the true author of the schism between the Latin and the Eastern Church.

Rome's first revenge is taken in the gravity and depth of her organizing spirit. What men are St. Sylvester, St. Damasus, St. Gregory the Great! With admirable courage, Rome labours for the conversion of the barbarians; she attaches them to herself; she makes them her clients, her subjects. The masterpiece of her policy was her alliance with the Carolingian house, and the bold stroke by which she revived in that family the Empire which had been dead for 300 years. The Church of Rome then lifts herself up, more powerful than ever, and again, for eight centuries more, becomes the centre of all Western politics and life.

At this point my task comes to an end, and you will entrust to others that of narrating to you the wonderful story of the feudal Church, its greatness and its abuses. Some other guide will then show you the reaction against these abuses, Protestantism in its turn dividing the Latin Church, and in a sense returning to the primitive conception of Jesus. Each of these great pages of history will have its own charm and its own lesson. That of which I have told you the tale is full of grandeur. We are impartial only towards the dead. As long as Catholicism was a hostile power, a danger to liberty and the human mind, it was right to contend against it. Still, when history is used as a weapon of war, it is never well told. Our age is the age of history, for it is the age of doubt as to matters of dogma: it is the age in which the enlightened mind, refusing to enter upon the discussion of systems, says to itself: "If, ever since the birth of reason, so many thousand creeds have claimed to set forth the whole truth, and those claims have always been adjudged to be vain, is it likely that I should be more fortunate than so many others, and that the truth should have waited for my coming to make its final self-revelation?" There is no final revelation: there is only a pathetic attempt of that poor disinherited creature, man, to make his fate tolerable. But the just inference from this is not disdain, but goodwill. Whoever thinks that he has anything to teach us as to our destiny and our end, ought to be welcome.

Recal to your memories the judicious and discreet advice of the Northumbrian chief to the assembly which was debating the adoption of the doctrine brought by the Roman missionaries:

"I will tell you, O King, what methinks man's life is like. Sometimes, when your hall is lit up for supper on a wild winter's evening, and warmed by a fire in the midst, a sparrow flies in by one door, takes shelter for a moment in the warmth, and then flies out again by another door, and is lost in the stormy darkness. No one in the hall sees the bird before it enters, nor after it has gone forth; it is only seen while it hovers near the fire. Even so, I ween, as to this brief span of our life in this world: what has gone before it, what will come after it—of this we know nothing. If the strange teacher can tell us, by all means let him be heard."[1]

Alas! the missionaries of Rome did not bring with them even the minimum of certainty with which the old Northumbrian chief, like the true sage which he was, resolved to be content. Happy

---

[1] Bede, *Hist. Eccles.* ii. 12. Translation given by Canon Bright, "Chapters of early English Church History," p. 116.

he who allows himself to fall asleep to the idle sound of the threats which formerly terrified the human conscience, and now ought only to lull it to rest. One thing alone is certain: the Fatherly smile which every now and then gleams through Nature, bearing witness that an Eye looks down upon us, that a Heart follows us. Let us beware of every absolute formula which may one day become an obstacle to the free development of our minds. There is no religious communion which does not still possess the gifts of life and of grace; but it is on condition that humble docility is followed by sympathetic adhesion. The metaphor of the regiment, which Clement of Rome originated, and which has since been so often repeated, must be absolutely given up.

It has been your will that I should recal to you the grandeur of Catholicism at its finest period. I thank you for it. Ties of childhood, the closest of all ties, bind me to Catholicism; and I am often tempted to say of it what Job said (at least in our Latin version), *Etiam si occiderit me in ipso sperabo.* This family is too large not to have a future before it still. The strange excesses to which during the last fifty years it has lent itself, this unparalleled Pontificate of Pius IX., the most astonishing in history, cannot come to a commonplace end. There will be thunders and lightnings such as always accompany the great days of God's judgments. And this old mother, who cannot die yet, will have much to do in order to remain still possible, still acceptable to those who have loved her. It may be that, to stay the progress of the modern thought which is her conqueror, she will have recourse to the arts of the sorceress, to words such as those which Balder murmured on his funeral pile. The Catholic Church is a woman: let us distrust the magic words of her agony. What if some day she rouses herself to say to us: "My children, all here below is but symbol and dream. The only thing that is clear in this world is a tiny ray of azure light which gleams across the darkness, and seems as if it were the reflection of a benevolent Will. Come to my bosom: forgetfulness is there. For those who want fetishes, I have fetishes: to whomsoever desires good works, I offer good works: for those who wish the intoxication of the heart, I have the milk of my breasts, which intoxicates. For whoso want love and hate also, I abound in both; and if any one desires irony, I pour it from a full cup. Come, one and all: the time of dogmatic sadness is past: I have music and incense for your burials, flowers for your weddings, the joyous welcome of my bells for your newly-born." Well, if she spoke thus, we should be sorely perplexed. But she will not speak thus.

Your great and glorious England has resolved the practical part of the problem. Just as it is impossible to find the theoretical solution of the religious question, is it easy to trace the line of conduct which in such matters the State and the individual ought to pursue. It is all summed up in one word, Liberty. What can be simpler? Faith cannot be prescribed: a man believes what he thinks to be true; and no one can hold as truth what his mind leads him, rightly or wrongly, to find untrue. To deny liberty of thought is a species of contradiction. But from liberty of thought to the right of saying what one thinks, is only a single step. For the right of all is the same: I have no right to forbid any man to express his opinion; no man has the right to forbid me to express mine. This is a theory which will appear very commonplace to the transcendental doctors who believe themselves to be in possession of absolute truth. But we have one great advantage over them. To be consistent, they are compelled to persecute; while to us it is permitted to be tolerant, —tolerant to all, even to those who, if they could, would not be tolerant to us. Yes, let us dare even this paradox: liberty is the best weapon against the enemies of liberty. Some say to us in all sincerity: "We accept liberty from you, because, in accordance with your principles, you owe it us; but you shall not have it from us, because we do not owe it you." Well, let us give them liberty notwithstanding, nor imagine that we shall be overreached in the bargain. No; liberty is the great dissolvent of all fanaticisms. When I claim liberty for my foe, for the man who would put me down if he had the power, I really offer him the most fatal of all gifts. I compel him to drink a strong draught that will turn his head, while I keep sober. Science presupposes the virile rule of liberty: fanaticism, superstition cannot bear it. We do more harm to dogmatism by treating it with implacable mildness than by persecuting it, for by this mildness we inculcate the principle which cuts up dogmatism by the root,—the principle, namely, that all metaphysical controversy is barren, and that, in this region of thought, truth is for each what he thinks that he can dimly discern. The essential thing is, not to silence this dangerous teaching, to hush that discordant voice, but so to educate the human mind as to enable the multitude to see the futility of these angry controversies. When this spirit becomes the atmosphere of society, fanaticism can no longer exist. It is conquered by the general yieldingness. If instead of ordering Polyeucte to the scaffold, the judge, with a smile and a friendly shake of the hand, had let him go, Polyeucte would not have persevered in his obstinacy; he might even have become a man of common sense, and lived to smile, in his old age, at the hot-headed folly of his youth.

DR. MARTINEAU'S ADDRESS.

DR. MARTINEAU'S ADDRESS.

At the close of the Lectures, the thanks of the Trustees were conveyed to M. Renan in the following Address by Dr. James Martineau:

M. RENAN: I sincerely wish that the Hibbert Trustees had selected as the organ of their final thanks to you some one whose word would be more adequate than mine to the eminence of the Lecturer and the interest of the occasion. I cannot, however, disobey them, sharing, as I do, their gratitude for a visit, of which the benefit to us has been rendered, I fear, at the cost of some suffering to you; and sharing also the delight of your hearers in following a series of historical sketches, at once constituted into a whole by a tissue of philosophical conceptions, and separately rich in picturesque colouring and dramatic situations, and presented with that marvellous charm of literary form, in the command of which the French are the first among European nations, and, may I not add, M. Renan among the French.

I know not how it may be with others; but to me the interest of these Lectures has been deepened by a number of resemblances which they suggested between the age which they depicted and our own. The break-up of traditional beliefs which you so powerfully described, the severance of the higher culture from the still recognized religion, are surely phenomena largely repeated in the modern European mind. The unsatisfied wants and eager tentatives which found expression in the ethics of the philosophical schools of the Empire, are evident again in the anxieties, and throughout the conflicts, and even behind the levities, of contemporary thought. The introduction of foreign gods into Roman recognition is not without its counterpart in our keener curiosity about foreign religions: if we do not reserve a niche for their divinities, we find a publisher for their sacred books, and use Paternoster Row as our Pantheon. During the ancient suspense of faith, the question seemed to lie between Hellenism and Judaism, as now we hear that the alternative is, Catholicism or Agnosticism. The answer of history then was, that the victory should belong to *neither* and yet to *both;* the Christianity which won the crown blending in itself what was universal in either. May we not predict a similar result to the strife of modern tendencies, and expect the emergence of some faith remote alike from mediæval orthodoxy and present negations; so that "neither in this mountain, nor yet at Jerusalem, will men worship the Father," but on some height of thought and piety veiled as yet in cloud?

These are, perhaps, fanciful analogies; for I am aware how illusory such historical parallels are apt to be. At all events, they suffice to show us that we are living in a *critical* age, which sifts the products of the past, rather than in a *creative* age, which takes the initiative of an original and affluent future. It is only in such an age that Lectures like these have an important place. They assume that Religion is a permanent and powerful element in human life; that it involves beliefs about the relations between finite things and the infinite; that these beliefs cannot be uniform and stationary through the changing contents of finite experience, and the changing capacity of thought for adjusting their relations; that it is of great importance to save religion from discordance with knowledge, by opening to it a possibility of movement *pari passu;* and that it is useful for this end to compare together religions of different source and different age, so as to obtain an insight into the human and historical conditions of their existence. Their opposite errors will thus cancel one another; and what is obsolete, what is partial, what is false in all, will withdraw in favour of whatever residual truth is enshrined within the withered husk. No doubt, we gain thus nothing but an eclectic result: but a critical age is incompetent to more; and, in doing this, prepares a clear space for the returning forces of the creative spirit.

For large help towards such preparations, accept, Monsieur, this expression of acknowledgment; and forgive its English *gaucherie*. I know, indeed, that I may rely on your benevolence to translate it into something better than it is; for in listening yesterday to the neat and elegant sentences that came through your lips from the feeble and unpolished Clement of Rome, I could not but feel that he had found a generous interpreter. I must pray you to extend the same grace to me, and translate my poor words into what I might have said, had I at command the Parisian language and culture of to-day. I need this indulgence: for, alas! I have lost all that I should have derived from France—the land of my forefathers—except my name and my descent, and, let me add, my ready homage to all such genius and learning as have placed M. Renan among her foremost scholars and most brilliant littérateurs.

WILLIAMS AND NORGATE'S PUBLICATIONS.

THE HIBBERT LECTURES, 1878.

Professor Max Müller's Lectures on the Origin and Growth of Religion, as illustrated by the Religions of India. Delivered in the Chapter House, Westminster Abbey, in April, May and June, 1878. By F. MAX MÜLLER. 8vo, cloth, 10s. 6d.

THE HIBBERT LECTURES, 1879.

Mr. Renouf's Lectures on the Origin and Growth of Religion, as illustrated by the Religion of Ancient Egypt. By P. LE PAGE RENOUF. 8vo, cloth, 10s. 6d.

The Resurrection of Jesus Christ. An Essay in Three Chapters. By REGINALD W. MACAN, Christ Church, Oxford. Published for the Hibbert Trustees. 8vo, cloth, 5s.

THEOLOGICAL TRANSLATION FUND LIBRARY.

A Series of Translations by which the best results of recent theological investigations on the Continent, conducted without reference to doctrinal considerations, and with the sole purpose of arriving at truth, will be placed within reach of English readers. Three Volumes 8vo annually, for a Guinea Subscription.

Works already Published.

1. Baur (F. C.) Church History of the First Three Centuries. Translated from the third German Edition. Edited by the Rev. ALLAN MENZIES. 2 vols. 8vo, 21s.

2. Keim (Th.) History of Jesus of Nazara. Considered in its connection with the National Life of Israel, and related in detail. (In 6 vols.) Vols. I. to IV. Translated by ARTHUR RANSOM and the Rev. E. M. GELDART. Each 10s. 6d.

3. Baur (F. C.) Paul, the Apostle of Jesus Christ, his Life and Work, his Epistles and Doctrine. A Contribution to a Critical History of Primitive Christianity. Second Edition. By Rev. ALLAN MENZIES. 2 vols. 21s.

4. Hausrath (A.) History of the New Testament Times. The Time of Jesus. By Dr. A. HAUSRATH, Professor of Theology, Heidelberg. Translated, with the Author's sanction, from the Second German Edition, by the Revds. C. T. POYNTING and P. QUENZER. 2 vols. 8vo, 21s.

5. Pfleiderer (Professor O.) of Jena. Paulinism: a Contribution to the History of Primitive Christian Theology. Translated by E. PETERS. 2 vols. 21s.

6. Kuenen (A.) The Religion of Israel to the Fall of the Jewish State. Translated by A. H. MAY. 3 vols. 8vo, 31s. 6d.

7. Ewald (H.) Commentary on the Prophets of the Old Testament. Translated by the Rev. J. FREDERICK SMITH. (In 5 vols.) Vols. I. to IV. Each 10s. 6d.

WILLIAMS AND NORGATE'S PUBLICATIONS.

THEOLOGICAL TRANSLATION FUND LIBRARY—continued.

8. Zeller (E.) The Acts of the Apostles Critically Examined. To which is prefixed, Overbeck's Introduction from De Wette's Handbook, translated by JOSEPH DARE. 2 vols. 8vo, 21s.

9. Bleek's Lectures on the Apocalypse. Edited by the Rev. Dr. S. DAVIDSON. 10s. 6d.

The price of the Works to Subscribers, 7s. per vol., £7. 7s.; to the Public, £11. 11s.

Works in the Press.

A Short Protestant Commentary on the New Testament; including Introductions to the Books, by Lipsius, Holsten, Lang, Pfleiderer, Holtzmann, Hilgenfeld and others. Translated by the Rev. F. H. JONES.

Ewald's Commentary on the Poetical Books of the Old Testament. Part I. The Psalms. Translated by the Rev. E. JOHNSON. (In 2 vols.)

The Fifth Volume of Keim's History of Jesus, translated by A. RANSOM; and

The Fifth and last Volume of Ewald's Prophets, translated by the Rev. J. FREDERICK SMITH.

Prospectus may be had on application.

The Bible for Young People. By Drs. OORT and HOOYKAAS, with with the assistance of Dr. A. KUENEN. Translated from the Dutch, with the sanction and assistance of the Authors, by PHILIP H. WICKSTEED, M.A. Complete in 6 vols. Crown 8vo, cloth, 31s.

Strauss (David F.) A New Life of Jesus; for the People. Authorized Translation. 2 vols. 8vo, cloth, 24s.

"On the present occasion I write especially for the use of laymen, and have taken particular pains that no single sentence shall be unintelligible to any educated or thoughtful person."—*Preface.*

Wright (Rev. J.) The Grounds and Principles of Religion. By Rev. JOHN WRIGHT, B.A. Crown 8vo, cloth, 5s.

Miss F. P. Cobbe. The Hopes of the Human Race, Hereafter and Here. Essays on the Life after Death, and the Evolution of the Social Sentiment. By FRANCES POWER COBBE. Second Edition. Crown 8vo, cloth, 5s.

Miss F. P. Cobbe. Broken Lights. An Inquiry into the Present Condition and Future Prospects of Religious Faith. Third Edition. Crown 8vo, cloth, 5s.

Martineau (Rev. Dr. James) Ideal Substitutes for God, considered in an Opening Lecture delivered October 30, 1878, at Manchester New College, London, 93rd Session. Third Edition. 8vo, 1s.

Martineau (Rev. Dr. James) Modern Materialism: its Attitude towards Theology. A Critique and Defence. Also, Religion as affected by Modern Materialism. Fifth Edition. 8vo, 2s. 6d.

SELECTED LIST

OF

WILLIAMS & NORGATE'S WORKS.

A **Study of the Saviour in the Newer Light;** or, A Present-day Study of Jesus Christ. By Alexander Robinson, B.D., formerly Minister of the Parish of Kilmun, Argyleshire. Second Edition, Revised and partly Re-written. Demy 8vo. 404 pp. 7s. 6d.

Semitic Influence in Hellenic Mythology. With special Reference to the Recent Mythological Works of Professor Max Müller and Mr. Andrew Lang. By Robert Brown, Junior, F.S.A., M.R.A.S., etc. Demy 8vo. cloth 7s. 6d.

Theological Translation Library.
NEW SERIES.

In the press, Vol. III. of the Third Year. Demy 8vo. 10s. 6d.

A HISTORY OF DOGMA.

Vol. IV. By Dr. Adolph Harnack, Ordinary Professor of Church History in the University, and Fellow of the Royal Academy of Science, Berlin. Translated from the Third German Edition by E. B. Speirs, D.D. Edited by Rev. A. B. Bruce, D.D.

Volumes V., VI. and VII. completing this work are in the Translator's hands.

Earlier Volumes of the New Series:

History of Dogma. Vols. I. and II. Translated from the Third German Edition by Rev. Neil Buchanan. Edited by Rev. Dr. A. B. Bruce, with a Preface specially written for this Edition by the Author. Vol. III. Translated by James Millar, B.D. 8vo. cloth.

Each 10s. 6d.

A History of the Hebrews. By R. Kittel, Ordinary Professor of Theology in the University of Breslau. Translated by the Revs. Hope W. Hogg, B.D., and E. B. Speirs, D.D. 2 vols. 8vo. cloth. Each 10s. 6d.

The Apostolic Age of the Christian Church. By Carl Von Weizsacker, Professor of Church History in the University of Tübingen. Translated from the Second and Revised Edition by James Millar, B.D. 2 vols. 8vo. cloth.

Each 10s. 6d.

The Communion of the Christian with God. A Discussion in agreement with the View of Luther. By W. Hermann, Professor of Dogmatic Theology in the University of Marburg. Translated from the Second German Edition, with Special Annotations by the Author, by J. Sandys Stanyon, M.A. 8vo. cloth   10s. 6d.

Theological Translation Fund Library.

FIRST SERIES.

The price of the Volumes of this Series is now reduced to 6s. per Volume.

THE SERIES COMPRISES:

BAUR (F. C.) Church History of the First Three Centuries. Translated from the Third German Edition. Edited by the Rev. Allan Menzies. 2 vols.   Each 6s.

BAUR (F. C.) Paul, the Apostle of Jesus Christ, his Life and Work, his Epistles and Doctrines. A Contribution to a Critical History of Primitive Christianity. Second Edition. By Rev. Allan Menzies. 2 vols.   Each 6s.

BLEEK'S Lectures on the Apocalypse. Edited by Rev. Dr. S. Davidson.   6s.

EWALD (H.) Commentary on the Prophets of the Old Testament. Translated by Rev. J. Frederick Smith. 5 vols. 8vo.   Each 6s.

EWALD (H.) Commentary on the Psalms. Translated by Rev. E. Johnson, M.A. 2 vols. 8vo.   Each 6s.

EWALD (H.) Commentary on the Book of Job, with Translation by Professor H. Ewald. Translated from the German by Rev. J. Frederick Smith. 1 vol. 8vo.   6s.

HAUSRATH (Professor A.) History of the New Testament Times. The Time of Jesus. By Dr. A. Hausrath, Professor of Theology, Heidelberg. Translated, with the Author's sanction, from the Second German Edition, by Revs. C. T. Poynting and P. Quenzer. 2 vols. 8vo.
     Each 6s.

KEIM (Th.) History of Jesus of Nazara. Considered in its connection with the National Life of Israel, and related in detail. Translated by Arthur Ransom and Rev. E. M. Geldart. 6 vols. 8vo.   Each 6s.
     Vol. I. will not be sold without Vols. II.-VI.

KUENEN (A.) The Religion of Israel to the Fall of the Jewish State. Translated by A. H. May. Second Edition. 3 vols. 8vo.   Each 6s.

PFLEIDERER (Professor O.) **The Philosophy of Religion on the Basis of its History.** Translated by Rev. Allan Menzies and Rev. Alex. Stewart, of Dundee. 4 vols. 8vo. cloth Each 6s.

PFLEIDERER (Professor O.) **Paulinism**; a Contribution to the History of Primitive Christian Theology. Translated by E. Peters. Second Edition. 2 vols. 8vo. Each 6s.

Protestant Commentary on the New Testament; with General and Special Introductions to the Books, by Lipsius, Holsten, Lang, Pfleiderer, Holtzman, Hilgenfeld, and others. Translated by Rev. F. H. Jones. 3 vols. 8vo. Each 6s.

REVILLE (Rev. Dr.) **Prolegomena of the History of Religion.** With Introduction by Professor Max Müller. 6s.

SCHRADER (Professor E.) **The Cuneiform Inscriptions and the Old Testament.** Translated by Rev. Owen C. Whitehouse. 2 vols. 8vo. Map Each 6s.

ZELLER (E.) **The Acts of the Apostles Critically Examined.** To which is prefixed Overbeck's Introduction from De Wette's Handbook. Translated by Joseph Dare. 2 vols. 8vo. Each 6s.

Uniform with the above Series.

HAUSRATH (A.) **History of the New Testament Times.** The Time of the Apostles. Translated by Leonard Huxley; with an Introduction by Mrs. Humphry Ward. 4 vols. 42s.

THE HIBBERT LECTURES.

Each Volume uniform in original binding. Demy 8vo. Cloth. 10s. 6d. Cheap Editions. Demy 8vo. Cloth. Price 3s. 6d. each. Uniform in style and binding.

1894.—Rev. Principal DRUMMOND. **Via, Veritas, Vita.** Lectures on Christianity in its most Simple and Intelligible Form. 2nd Edition.

1893.—Rev. C. B. UPTON, B.A. Lectures on the Bases of Religious Belief.

1892.—C. G. MONTEFIORE. Lectures on the Origin and Growth of Religion as illustrated by the Religion of the Ancient Hebrews. 3rd Edition.

1891.—Count GOBLET d'ALVIELLA. Lectures on the Evolution of the Idea of God. Translated by Rev. P. H. Wicksteed. 2nd Edition.

1888.—Rev. Dr. HATCH. Lectures on the Influence of Greek Ideas and Usages upon the Christian Church. Edited by Dr. Fairbairn. 7th Edition.

1887.—Professor A. H. SAYCE. Lectures on the Religion of Ancient Assyria and Babylonia. 4th Edition.

1886.—Professor J. RHYS. Lectures on the Origin and Growth of Religion as illustrated by Celtic Heathendom. 3rd Edition.

1885.—Professor PFLEIDERER. Lectures on the Influence of the Apostle Paul on the Development of Christianity. Translated by the Rev. J. Frederick Smith. 3rd Edition.

1884.—Professor ALBERT REVILLE. Lectures on the Ancient Religions of Mexico and Peru. 2nd Edition.

1883.—The Rev. CHARLES BEARD. Lectures on the Reformation of the Sixteenth Century in its Relation to Modern Thought and Knowledge. 3rd Edition.

1882.—Professor KUENEN. Lectures on National Religions and Universal Religions. 3rd Edition.

1881.—T. W. RHYS DAVIDS. Lectures on the Origin and Growth of Religion as Illustrated by some Points in the History of Indian Buddhism. 3rd Edition.

1880.—M. ERNEST RENAN. Lectures on the Influence of the Institutions, Thought and Culture of Rome on Christianity, and the Development of the Catholic Church. Translated by the Rev. Charles Beard. 4th Edition.

1897.—P. LE PAGE RENOUF. Lectures on the Religion of Ancient Egypt. 2nd Edition.

Works published for the Hibbert Trustees.

WALLIS (H. W.) The Cosmology of the Rig-Veda. 8vo. cloth. 5s.

POOLE (R. L.) Illustrations of the History of Mediæval Thought in the Departments of Theology and Ecclesiastical Politics. 8vo. cloth. 10s. 6d.

STOKES (G. J.) The Objectivity of Truth. 8vo. cloth. 5s.

EVANS (G.) An Essay of Assyriology. With an Assyrian Tablet in Cuneiform type. 8vo. cloth. 5s.

SCHURMAN (J. G.) Kantian Ethics and the Ethics of Evolution. A Critical Study. 8vo. cloth. 5s.

MACAN (R. W.) The Resurrection of Jesus Christ. An Essay, in Three Chapters. 8vo. cloth. 5s.

WICKSTEED (P. H.) The Ecclesiastical Institutions of Holland, treated with special reference to the Position and Prospects of the Modern School of Theology. 8vo. 1s.

ALVIELLA (Count Goblet d') The Contemporary Evolution of Religious Thought in England, America, and India. Translated from the French by the Rev. J. Moden. 8vo. cloth. 10s. 6d.

BARNABAS' Epistle, in Greek, from the Sinaitic Manuscript of the Bible, with a Translation by S. Sharpe. Crown 8vo. cloth. 2s. 6d.

BAYNES (H.) The Idea of God and the Moral Sense in the light of Language; being a philological Enquiry into the rise and growth of Spiritual and Moral Concepts. 8vo. cloth. 10s. 6d.

BEARD (Rev. Dr. C.) The Universal Christ, and other Sermons. Crown 8vo. cloth. 7s. 6d.

—— Port Royal. A Contribution to the History of Religion and Literature in France. Cheap Edition. 2 vols. Crown 8vo. cloth. 12s.

BEARD (Rev. Dr. John R.) The Autobiography of Satan. Crown 8vo. cloth. 7s. 6d.

Bible, translated by Samuel Sharpe, being a Revision of the Authorized English Version. 6th Edition of the Old, 10th Edition of the New Testament. 8vo. roan. 5s.

CHANNING'S Complete Works, including "The Perfect Life," with a Memoir. Centennial Edition. 848 pp. 8vo. cloth. 2s.

CLARK (Archd. Jas.) De Successione Apostolica nec non Missione et Jurisdictione Hierarchiae Anglicanae et Catholicae. 8vo. (*Georgetown, Guiana.*) Cloth. 21s.

—— Seven Ages of the Church; or Exposition of the Apocalypse. Sewed. 1s.

Common Prayer for Christian Worship: in Ten Services for Morning and Evening. 32mo. cloth. 1s. 6d. Also in 8vo. cloth. 3s.

DRUMMOND (Dr.) Philo Judæus; or, the Jewish Alexandrian Philosophy in its Development and Completion. By James Drummond, LL.D., Principal of Manchester New College, Oxford. 2 vols. 8vo. cloth. 21s.

Echoes of Holy Thoughts; arranged as Private Meditations before a First Communion. 2nd Edition, with a Preface by Rev. J. Hamilton Thom. Printed with red lines. Fcap. 8vo. cloth. 1s.

FIGG (E. G.) Analysis of Theology, Natural and Revealed. Crown 8vo. cloth. 6s.

FOUR Gospels, The, as Historical Records. 8vo. cloth. 15s.

FUERST (Dr. Jul.) Hebrew and Chaldee Lexicon to the Old Testament. 5th Edition, improved and enlarged. Translated by Rev. Dr. Samuel Davidson. Royal 8vo. cloth. 21s.

GILL (C.) The Evolution of Christianity. By Charles Gill. 2nd edition. With Dissertations in Answer to Criticism. 8vo. cloth. 12s.

GILL (C.) The Book of Enoch the Prophet. Translated from an Ethiopic MS. in the Bodleian Library, by the late Richard Laurence, LL.D., Archbishop of Cashel. The Text corrected from his latest Notes by Charles Gill. Re-issue, 8vo. cloth. 5s.

GOULD (Rev. S. Baring) Lost and Hostile Gospels. An account of the Toledoth Jesher, two Hebrew Gospels circulating in the Middle Ages, and Extant Fragments of the Gospels of the first Three Centuries of Petrine and Pauline Origin. Crown 8vo. cloth. 7s. 6d.

HARDY (R. Spence) Manual of Buddhism in its Modern Development. Translated from Singhalese MSS. 2nd Edition, with a complete Index and Glossary. 8vo. cloth. 21s.

HAUSRATH (A.) History of the New Testament Times. The Time of the Apostles. Translated by Leonard Huxley; with an Introduction by Mrs. Humphry Ward. 4 vols. 42s.

Hebrew Texts, in large type for Classes :
Genesis. 2nd Edition. 16mo. cloth. 1s. 6d.
Psalms. 16mo. cloth. 1s.
Isaiah. 16mo. cloth. 1s.
Job. 16mo. cloth. 1s.

HEMANS (Chas. I.) Historic and Monumental Rome. A Handbook for the Students of Classical and Christian Antiquities in the Italian Capital. Crown 8vo. cloth. 10s. 6d.

HOERNING (Dr. R.) The Karaite MSS., British Museum. The Karaite Exodus (i. to viii. 5) in 42 Autotype Facsimiles, with a Transcription in ordinary Arabic type. Together with Descriptions and Collation of that and five other MSS. of Portions of the Hebrew Bible in Arabic Characters in the same Collection. Royal 4to. cloth, gilt top. £2. 12s. 6d.

JONES (Rev. R. Crompton) Hymns of Duty and Faith, selected and arranged. 247 pp. Foolscap 8vo. cloth. 2nd Edition. 3s. 6d.

—————— **Chants, Psalms, and Canticles,** selected and pointed for Chanting. 18mo. cloth. 1s. 6d.

—————— **Anthems,** with Indexes and References to the Music. 18mo. cloth. 1s. 3d.

—————— **The Chants and Anthems,** together in one vol. Cloth. 2s.

—————— **A Book of Prayer,** in Thirty Orders of Worship, with Additional Prayers and Thanksgivings. 18mo. cloth. 2s. 6d.

—————— The same, with Chants, in one vol. 18mo. cloth. 3s.

KENNEDY (Rev. Jas.) Introduction to Biblical Hebrew, presenting Graduated Instruction in the Language of the Old Testament. By James Kennedy, B.D., Acting Librarian in the New College, and one of the additional Examiners in Divinity at the University, Edinburgh. 8vo. cloth. 12s.

——— Studies in Hebrew Synonyms. 5s.

MALAN (Rev. Dr. S. C.) The Book of Adam and Eve, also called the Conflict of Adam and Eve with Satan. A Book of the Early Eastern Church. Translated from the Ethiopic, with Notes from the Kufale, Talmud, Midrashim, and other Eastern Works. 8vo. cloth. 7s. 6d.

MALAN (Rev. Dr. S. C.) Original Notes on the Book of Proverbs. According to the Authorized Version. Vol. I. Chap. i. to x. 8vo. cloth. 12s.
Vol. II. Chap. xi. to xx. 8vo. cloth. 12s.
Vol. III. Chap. xxi. to xxxi. 8vo. cloth. 12s.

MARTINEAU (Rev. Dr. James) The Relation between Ethics and Religion. An Address. 8vo. sewed. 1s.

MARTINEAU (Prof. Russell) The Roots of Christianity in Mosaism. 8vo. sewed. 1s.

MASSEY (Gerald) A Book of the Beginnings. Containing an Attempt to recover and reconstitute the lost Origines of the Myths and Mysteries, Types and Symbols, Religion and Language, with Egypt for the Mouthpiece and Africa as the Birthplace. 2 vols. Imperial 8vo. cloth. 30s.

——— **The Natural Genesis;** or Part the Second of "A Book of the Beginnings." 2 vols. Imperial 8vo. cloth. 30s.

Our Christian Creed. 2nd and greatly Revised Edition. Crown 8vo. cloth. 3s. 6d.

PERRIN (R. S.) Religion of Philosophy, the, or the Unification of Knowledge: a Comparison of the chief Philosophical and Religious Systems of the World. 8vo. cloth. 16s.

QUARRY (Rev. J.) Genesis and its Authorship. Two Dissertations. 2nd Edition, with Notice of Animadversions of the Bishop of Natal. 8vo. cloth. 12s.

SADLER (Rev. Dr.) Prayers for Christian Worship. Crown 8vo. cloth. 3s. 6d.

——— **Closet Prayers,** Original and Compiled. 18mo. cloth. 1s. 6d.

SAVAGE (M. J.) Beliefs about the Bible. 8vo. cloth. 7s. 6d.

SHARPE (Samuel) History of the Hebrew Nation and its Literature. With an Appendix on the Hebrew Chronology. 5th Edition. Crown 8vo. cloth. 4s. 6d.

——— **Critical Notes** on the Authorized English Version of the New Testament. 2nd Edition. 12mo. cloth. 1s. 6d.

SHARPE (Samuel) Short Notes to accompany a Revised Translation of the Hebrew Scriptures. 12mo. cloth. 1s. 6d.

STRAUSS (Dr. D. F.) Life of Jesus; for the People. The Authorized English Edition. 2 vols. 8vo. cloth. 10s. 6d.

SUFFIELD. Life of the Rev. Robert Rodolph, Author of "The Crown of Jesus." Photogravure Portrait. Crown 8vo. cloth. 4s. 6d.

TAUCHNITZ'S English New Testament. Authorized Version; with Introduction, and various Readings from the three most celebrated Manuscripts of the Original Greek Text. By C. Tischendorf. 12mo. sewed, 1s. 6d.; cloth, 2s.

TAYLER (Rev John James) An Attempt to ascertain the Character of the Fourth Gospel, especially in its relation to the first Three. 2nd Edition. 8vo. cloth. 5s.

Testament, the New. Translated from Griesbach's Text by S. Sharpe, Author of "The History of Egypt." 14th Thousand. Fcap. 8vo. cloth. 1s. 6d.

VICKERS (J.) History of Herod; or, Another Look at a Man emerging from Twenty Centuries of Calumny. Crown 8vo. cloth. 6s.

―――― **The Real Jesus;** a Review of his Life, Character, and Death, from a Jewish Standpoint. Crown 8vo. 6s.

―――― **The Crucifixion Mystery.** Crown 8vo. cloth. 3s. 6d.

WRIGHT (Rev. C. H. H.) Book of Genesis in Hebrew Text. With a critically revised Text, various Readings, and Grammatical and Critical Notes. Demy 8vo. Reduced to 3s. 6d.

―――― **Book of Ruth** in Hebrew Text. With a critically revised Text, various Readings, including a new Collation of Twenty-eight Hebrew MSS., and a Grammatical and Critical Commentary; to which is appended, The Chaldee Targum. Demy 8vo. 7s. 6d.

WRIGHT (G. H. Bateson, D.D.) The Book of Job. A new critically revised Translation, with Essays on Scansion, Date, etc. 8vo. cloth. 6s.

Was Israel ever in Egypt? or, a Lost Tradition. By G. H. Bateson Wright, D.D., Queen's College, Oxford; Headmaster Queen's College, Hong Kong. 8vo. linen. 7s. 6d.

"A contribution of considerable weight to the literature of the higher criticism. The work is one which well deserves the attention of all serious students of the higher criticism, and while it sums up and confirms some conclusions of prior critics, it has an original and independent value as offering a new theory of the Exodus. It is a carefully reasoned and acute book, which will add to its author's already high reputation as a critic of the Scriptures."—*Scotsman*.

WRIGHT (Rev. J.) Grounds and Principles of Religion. Crown 8vo. cloth. 3s.

www.ingramcontent.com/pod-product-compliance
Lightning Source LLC
Chambersburg PA
CBHW020812230426
43666CB00007B/976